THRIFT STORE

THRIFT STORE

SAInts

Meeting Jesus
25¢ at a Time

JANE F. KNUTH

LOYOLAPRESS.
A JESUIT MINISTRY
Chicago

LOYOLA PRESS.
A JESUIT MINISTRY

3441 N. Ashland Avenue
Chicago, Illinois 60657
(800) 621-1008
www.loyolapress.com

Many of the stories in *Thrift Store Saints* were published in part or in full in *The Good News*, the newsletter for the Roman Catholic Diocese of Kalamazoo, dioceseofkalamazoo.org/communication. Chapter 3 was previously published in *St. Anthony Messenger Magazine* (October 2001). Reprinted by permission of St. Anthony Messenger Press, 28 W. Liberty St., Cincinnati, OH 45202. 800-488-0488. www.americancatholic.org. All rights reserved. Chapters 8 and 15 were previously published in *Catholic Digest* (December 2003 and November 2006). Chapters 6, 7, and 15 were previously published in *The Ozanam News* (1st Quarter, 2007). Permission is gratefully acknowledged.

Quotes from Frédéric Ozanam and St. Vincent de Paul are from *Manual of the Society of St. Vincent de Paul.*

Cover images: (wp) stacked coins, © Karen Beard, Getty Images; (cl) rosary, © Paul Maguire, istockphoto.com; (ul) S, © Louis Rice; (ul) A, © Harvey Lloyd, Getty Images; (um) I, © Ronald P. Ziolkowski Jr., Flickr, Getty Images; (um), N, © Darrell Gulin, Getty Images; (ur) t, © Leo Reynolds, Flickr, www.leoreynolds.co.uk; (ur) s, © Leo Reynolds, Flickr, www.leoreynolds.co.uk; Back cover images: (ul) J, © takomabibelot, Flickr

Library of Congress Cataloging-in-Publication Data
Knuth, Jane.
Thrift store saints : meeting Jesus 25 cents at a time / Jane Knuth.
    p. cm.
ISBN-13: 978-0-8294-3301-2
ISBN-10: 0-8294-3301-5
1. Church work with the poor--Catholic Church. 2. Society of St. Vincent de Paul.
3. Christian life--Catholic authors. 4. Spirituality--Catholic Church. I. Title.
BX2347.8.P66K58 2010
261.8'325088282--dc22

                                                                    2010020023

Printed in the United States of America
17 18 19 20 21 22 Versa 14 13 12 11 10 9

For Dean

A NOTE FROM
THE AUTHOR

All of the stories in this book are true. However, the St. Vincent de Paul Society strictly guards the privacy of the individuals whom we help. In keeping with this, I changed names, occupations, physical descriptions, and details of the assistance we rendered. Any resulting resemblance to other persons is coincidental and unintentional. Peoples' problems are rarely unique, but their goodness always is—that is where the disguises may fail. I ask for forgiveness if that is the case. There are a few instances in which I received permission to tell a story without changes, and I am grateful for these generous souls.

CONTENTS

PREFACE

Thirteen years ago I reluctantly volunteered to work at a St. Vincent de Paul thrift store on a temporary basis because they were a little short of helpers. Right away, curious incidents that were almost like grace started to occur. Like grace, but not quite. It felt like something that would be grace very soon, if only I would keep coming back.

Thrift Store Saints is about recognizing God among us when the language is rough, the labor seems mindless, and everybody is wearing old clothes. God is certainly in the bread and the wine, and in the Gospels and the Epistles. He is in the organ preludes, the processions, the incense, sometimes in the sermons, and always in the fellowship of believers. But six out of seven days he is raking leaves, visiting sick babies, giving away the day-old bread, and handling the money.

The "Rule," or spiritual path, of the St. Vincent de Paul Society can be summarized in three steps:

1. Pray together.
2. Help poor people face-to-face.
3. The poor are our teachers.

We are their students. As a student of Vincentian spirituality, this book is my midterm. I hope and pray that my teachers, the poor, will grade on a curve.

IS THIS A CHURCH?

Three people are waiting on the sidewalk in the drizzle. I drive past them and around the end of the building.

As I park my car next to the fresh graffiti, I chew on my lip and say to myself for the hundredth time, *What are you doing here, Jane? You don't know the first thing about helping poor people.* I climb out of the warm car, put my purse in the trunk, and lock all the doors. In the midst of my anxiety, I remind myself what I've been taught. *This isn't social work; it's a spiritual path. Those three people standing outside aren't problems to be solved— they are my teachers. They aren't going to mug me—they're going to show me the way to God.*

I consider retrieving my purse out of the trunk. But I don't. I stick my hands in my pockets and walk around the corner of the building.

"Morning," I greet them as I fit the key in the door.

The youngest man cups his hands around his eyes and peers through the plate glass window at the racks of clothing, mismatched dishes, and blankets, and asks me, "Is this a church? My worker at the Department of Human Services gave me the address. They told me

St. Vincent de Paul, but this looks like some kind of store. Am I in the right place?"

"No, it's not a church, and yes, you're in the right place. Do you need help with something?"

He nods. "The electric bill."

They are all nodding.

"The rent."

"They shut off my water."

"It will be just a few minutes." As I open the door, I apologize for the foul weather and explain that I can't let them inside until more of the volunteer staff arrives. I have lengthened their miserable wait, but no one complains. They shrug and shiver.

The store is cold, but the furnace begins to seek its daytime temperature. I hang up my coat as my coworkers arrive. Before I unlock the door, we pause and clasp our hands together for a prayer to start the day. We're not very pious at the St. Vincent de Paul Society. Usually our prayers are seat-of-the-pants petitions, no preambles and no qualifiers; people are waiting in the rain after all. "Lord, we need money." "God, give me patience." "Help us to listen better." "Don't let the roof leak again."

The work of the St. Vincent de Paul Society lies smack in the middle of this drizzly, impious world. We are out on the front lines doing that confusing Beatitude thing without Roman collars or mission statements. That is what being "laity" is all about; it's about the other six days, the ones that God called "good."

The seventh day he called "holy" and we focus on worship, study, and celebration for that reason, but there is also something of God to be found in the rest of the week. This book is about the other six days, stories of God on the job and on the street.

"Is this a church?"

Maybe it is.

1

DOROTHY

The first day I walk into the St. Vincent de Paul shop I am there for a quick in and out. I need to buy a rosary for my daughter's First Communion, and this is the only local place that sells them. The limited operating hours of the store have foiled me twice already on this mission, but at last, I have caught them before they close at 3:00 p.m.

The tiny, white-haired lady behind the counter helps me select a rosary, a satin case, and a prayer book. She bags them for me, totals up my purchase on the register, and then balks at my offered credit card.

"I'm so sorry," she says. "We don't take those."

I know this can't be right. Every store in town takes credit cards. McDonald's takes credit cards. I offer her a different card, but she isn't fooling around.

"Would you have cash or a check, perhaps?" she asks.

"Look," I tell her. "This is the third time I've driven downtown. Your hours are lousy. What are working people supposed to do? I teach, and I have children in school, but you close at three o'clock. Now you're telling me you won't take credit cards? This is ridiculous."

She nods sympathetically. "Most of our customers don't have credit cards. So usually it's not a problem."

I am pretty sure she is making this up. At this stage in my life I don't realize that there are people in the world who don't have credit cards. I begin to look around me suspiciously.

The little shop is a one-story concrete block structure with three large plate glass windows. The main room where I am standing is about the size of two garages. The center floor space is dedicated to tightly packed used-clothing racks. Floor-to-ceiling shelves line the three windowless walls and are crammed with cast-off household items. Where I am standing, in the front of the store near the windows, six glass-front display cases surround the cash register, showing off brand new rosaries, prayer books, Bibles, medals, and crucifixes. The shiny religious gifts contrast oddly with the clutter of used merchandise. It's as if someone set up a chapel inside a garage sale. Something isn't right.

Could this place be a front for illegal activity? Maybe this little old lady isn't really selling rosaries at all. Maybe this is really a cover for some other kind of action.

The neighborhood certainly fits the bill. There is a homeless shelter across the street, two vacant, boarded-up houses next door, train tracks half a block away, a funeral home kitty-corner across the intersection and, last, a prosperous-looking firm dealing with electronic security systems across from that.

I am on the point of leaving the merchandise on the counter and announcing that I intend to shop elsewhere when a very large man pushes his way through the front door and points a finger directly at the cashier in front of me. He is big of voice and beard, but small of manners and cleanliness.

"I need shoes to wear to church," he announces in a loud, slurring voice. "These here you gave me yesterday ain't nice enough for church going," he says as he looks in the direction of his feet.

We all look. The unholy shoes appear to be gently worn loafers, and they are approaching the counter in an indirect saunter. As they waft nearer, so does the thick smell of recently consumed alcohol.

I take two voluntary steps backward, giving him plenty of room. He towers ten inches above me, which is reason enough to yield the right-of-way, but his entire person is daunting in itself. There are deep lines running from his nostrils to the corners of his mouth, which blend into the fuzziness of a stubbly jaw. His square shoulders balance well with thick salt-and-pepper hair and, if not for the obvious substance-abuse issue going on, here would be a man who is at his most impressive stage of life.

He's still impressive. Just not in a positive way.

The tiny, elderly clerk smiles the same sympathetic smile at this smelly giant that she has just been directing so patiently at me and says, "Now, sir, those shoes are perfectly good for church. We talked about that yesterday when you picked them out, remember? My husband used to wear ones just like them to Mass on Sundays."

His thighs bump into the counter and for a moment it looks like he might pitch over on top of her. Then he slaps his palms down next to my daughter's rosary beads and catches his balance by leaning his weight on the counter.

At this point, the alcohol smell is no longer covering the rest of the aroma coming from him. I switch to mouth breathing. In my peripheral vision I see other customers start to edge toward the door. My path is blocked for that route. I move around the end of the counter in order to put something solid between us, and find myself practically standing next to the cashier.

She smiles reassuringly at me and pats my hand and says to the man, "We give shoes out twice a year, you know that. You can come back in September and we'll help you again."

The large, drunken man is now a large, drunken, angry man. He pounds one of his fists on the counter and rages about the charitable inadequacies and small-mindedness of the St. Vincent de Paul Society (I am paraphrasing, of course). "Tell the manager I want to see him! I'm not putting up with this no more 'cause I need shoes for church and you people call yourselves Christians and you don't give me any and that ain't right!"

I tug on the little lady's sleeve and whisper, "Should I call 911?"

She shakes her head at me and says calmly to the man, "Sir, I'm sorry you're upset. I only wish we could help, but shoes are in such short supply."

I am practically cowering behind the counter, glancing around for a way to defend myself and the clerk. I snatch up a ministapler and hide it in my palm.

"I want a manager! All I'm asking for are proper shoes to be seen in the house of God and you people don't give me nothing!"

She tries to reason with him, but drunken people lack those sorts of skills. Finally, she says, "How about if you come back tomorrow and I'm sure a manager will have time to see you then."

He breathes fumes into her face and shouts, "What's your name? I'm coming back tomorrow and I'm telling your boss exactly how you treat people. Tell me your name!"

"Oh," she waves her hand gently. "You'll never remember my name, sir. I'm nobody important anyway. You just come back tomorrow. I'm sure everything will work out."

To my utter astonishment, he gives up. Her unshakable kindness is too much for him. He grumbles and swears and waves his arms some more but in the end, he turns and shuffles his way out of the store.

In the silence that follows, the remaining customers poke their heads out from behind the clothing racks and ask, "Is he gone?"

I say to the clerk, "Do you want me to lock the door?"

She hesitates, then nods. "Maybe for a little while. I don't really care to talk with him again right away." She hands me the key, and I go to turn the bolt while another customer peers out the plate glass and gives us a running description of where the man is headed.

When I get back to the cash register, my daughter's rosary, satin case, and prayer book are still lying innocently on the counter.

The cashier frowns at the articles in a concerned way and says, "I could loan you the money for these if you want to bring it in next week. Let me just check my purse to see if I have enough with me."

I blink. She can't mean it. "You don't want to say things like that," I whisper to her and glance over my shoulder to see if any of the other customers overheard her.

She waves a hand unconcernedly and says, "Oh, I'm not worried. I'm sure you'll bring in the money. No one would walk away with a rosary and a prayer book without paying for them."

I study her solemnly. "I'd probably go straight to hell for that, wouldn't I?"

She laughs gently and winks at me.

I scrounge around in the bottom of my purse looking for paper money and coins, no longer grumbling about the three trips I have made. Eventually I find enough money to cover the bill and I hand it to her. She smiles, thanks me, and says, "Our hours are limited because we don't have enough volunteers right now. You wouldn't have any extra time to help out, would you?"

It's 1995, her name is Dorothy, she is eighty-two years old, and she will volunteer at the store twice a week for another thirteen years. She will become one of my best friends, but right now I am only trying to think how I can gracefully get out of helping in this crazy place with rosary beads and free shoes and drunken street people and white-haired, hundred-pound saints. Being Catholic, I'm all for martyrs, but not as a personal vocation. Luckily I have not signed a credit card slip or given them a check. No one here knows my name or my phone number; it's still possible to escape with my anonymity intact.

As I back away and mumble about "busy schedules" and "young children," she smiles sweetly at me and says, "Don't I know your Aunt Catherine? She and I were schoolmates together."

So much for anonymity.

2

LOSING MY BALANCE

The next week I am sitting in the back room of the store in a circle of nine elderly women. Dorothy's white hair is no anomaly; every member of the St. Vincent de Paul Society is over seventy. I am thirty-seven.

I agreed to *attend* this meeting. That's all. I have joined no organization, signed no papers, taken no vows, and exchanged no recipes. My purse is locked in my car, and I purposely did not bring pen or paper with me. I sit with my feet flat on the floor and politely refuse Dorothy's offer of coffee.

To Dorothy's left sits Mary, one of the cashiers. She is a feisty Croatian with beautiful white hair and a bad case of arthritic hands. Mary introduces me to Rosemary and Virginia on her left, both of them quiet but friendly enough. A jolly lady next to Virginia (I don't catch her name) who doesn't work in the store but visits people in nursing homes as her contribution to the group, shakes my hand vigorously and welcomes me. Sitting across the circle from her are two Bernies and an Alice. Everyone keeps talking about another Bernie, the president of the Society who only recently retired from volunteering. This confusion of Bernies messes with my mind for most of the next hour.

Alice, as the secretary of the group, asks Mary to read a prayer. After that, she leads off the meeting with the first order of business, which is to figure out who will be the next president. A few nominations are submitted and politely refused. Everyone claims ignorance of the duties involved. It doesn't take long before it's obvious that absolutely no one wants the job. Dorothy looks at me and smiles in that sweet way that roped me into attending this meeting, but there is no way. I've been on enough church committees in the past to know when it's a good time to sit on my hands and avoid eye contact.

Apparently, the absent Bernie resigned in a hurry without training anyone and left no instructions behind. No one wants to talk about the circumstances of her departure, but the upshot of it is that they are stuck with no leader and no candidates to take over.

I look around the circle of gray and white heads and ask them, "Why aren't there any people my age?"

"They all have jobs," is the collective opinion. "Baby boomers have no time for volunteering."

Well, jobs or not, all my friends seem to be volunteering around the clock—coaching sports; fund-raising for schools; organizing charity golf outings, phone-a-thons and walk-a-thons, raffles and auctions, Girl Scouts, Boy Scouts, 4-H, political campaigns, environmental clean-ups, carpools, and vacation bible school. They all have at least one no-pay job on top of their other commitments. But why are none of them at the local Catholic charity?

And my generation isn't the only one missing. Where are the Gen Xers? And what about the college and high school students? Why are these elderly volunteers all alone running a thrift store on the seedy side of town, and how can this possibly work? They simply can't do this all by themselves. Add to this the lack of leadership, and I begin to worry that they will expect way too much from me if I join. All the headaches of running a church group will fall on my shoulders because I am young and strong and competent.

Along with the memory of the drunken customer, nightmarish images of committee meetings, fund-raisers, volunteer recruitment fairs, negative balance sheets, recognition luncheons, bake sales, and phone trees appear in my imagination. I am already searching my pockets for my car keys when someone asks for a report from the treasurer.

Alice, the secretary, is also the treasurer of the group. She reads the minutes of the last meeting and ends with the current bank balance. This is when the second crisis arises. Due to a lack of volunteers, the income from the store has been building up, and they haven't been able to give it away fast enough. Alice announces that they are fifty thousand dollars in the black, which leads all of them to cluck their tongues in disapproval.

I am dumbfounded.

I have never in my life heard of a church group that is overfunded. I think that they must have the figures reversed, but no, these nine ladies really have generated more money than they have been able to spend.

"What are you going to do with all that money?" I ask.

One of the Bernies frowns grimly and says, "We are going to give it away as fast as we can." Everyone in the circle nods in agreement, and a discussion begins.

Virginia, who is ninety-something, explains to me, "The St. Vincent de Paul Society visits people in their homes to find out what they need. Our problem is that most of us don't like to drive into the rough neighborhoods after dark, and in the winter the sun goes down at five thirty."

I stare at her, appalled at the idea of her driving at all, let alone at night in the inner city.

"Perhaps we should stop taking donations for a while," Rosemary suggests.

But nobody likes that option very well.

Dorothy says, "Maybe we can ask people who need help to come here to the store?"

Bernie shakes her head. "We really should visit them in their own homes. That's how the Society is supposed to function. It gives people more dignity to have us come to them."

But lately, home visits haven't been possible for this tiny group who call themselves Vincentians, and meanwhile they keep right on generating income through the thrift store operation and donations from benefactors. Fifty thousand dollars is an embarrassment of riches for these daughters of the Great Depression. They are determined to give it away—but how?

In the end, they decide to put the word out in town among the various churches and help-agencies that they will begin to hold office hours for people seeking financial assistance.

"We'll write checks as fast as we can," Bernie promises everyone.

It's been said that the giant redwood trees in California don't die in the usual way. They don't get sick or weaken with age. Instead, what happens is that a perfectly healthy tree, on a windless day, with no disease or rot or even the excuse of a lightning strike, will lose its balance and topple over—*ca-thunk.* Tree experts speculate that there is a weakness in the roots, but no one knows for sure what causes these sudden deaths.

Understandably, this is distressing to tree lovers.

People often speak of "fallen-away Catholics." It's been said that their numbers in the United States would make up the second-largest denomination of Christians in the country. I've known a few self-described members of this group. It's as if these missing brethren are like untouched redwoods, suddenly careening to the forest floor for no good or apparent reason. People pray for their return to an upright position, but no one seems to understand what causes the phenomenon.

Understandably, this is distressing to church lovers.

I am a baby boomer. My generation knows how to fix the world like no one else. That's how we grew up. We were told to get an education and then go out and "make a difference." "Question authority," was our mantra. "Never follow blindly." We were all born to be leaders— not a follower in the bunch. Many of us Catholic boomers are still committed to changing the world, but not always from a position inside the Church. We are busy saving the environment, advocating societal reforms, standing up for human rights, and protesting injustice, but our concerns tend to be rooted more in the earth than the heavens. Many of my generation, good committed activists, no longer attend church. There are fallen tree trunks all around me.

At my first St. Vincent de Paul meeting, listening to the surreal discussion of how to give money away faster, it dawns on me that I have a lot more to offer the group than just an extra pair of hands to sort clothing. Talk revolves around (and around and around) routine management issues within the thrift store operation. How should we standardize prices? Shall we allow customers use of the restroom? Should we have a bag sale to reduce the inventory? Who keeps moving the scissors?

While the St. Vincent de Paul members discuss mundane matters like pricing tags and osteoporosis, I am already planning how to rip out the green shag carpet in the office and rev up the recruitment of new members. But first, it's obvious to me that what the place needs most is someone who can organize things better. Merchandise on the store shelves looks cluttered, the clothing racks are too tightly packed, the tiny office contains files going back two decades, and the entire place smells like a Michigan basement. I pride myself that I am very good at organization, and this is a talent that I can generously share.

Near the end of the meeting, I clear my throat and set the new course for the group with my first revolutionary suggestion. "What we need to do is to organize all the paperwork with a computer system. Once I get that in place, we can use it for inventory control, paying bills, client files, and make it possible for customers to use credit cards for purchases."

They look at me blankly and look at each other knowingly.

One of the octogenarians actually rolls her eyes. "That's nice, dear," she says. "But what we could really use is someone who would take out the trash every night and clean the bathroom."

I smile thinly at her while my mind reels with the insult. How is cleaning the bathroom going to change the world? That is not my idea of volunteer work. I can clean bathrooms at home if I want. It is a waste of my intellect, my education, my organizational skills, and my zeal to expect me to do such work. No wonder these people have no young volunteers. Perhaps it's time to pack up my leadership talents and leave this group with their ugly carpet and their wads of cash. If there is a weakness in my tree roots, it's their fault for not valuing my strengths.

But Dorothy, having gotten me this far, isn't letting go so easily. "What we could really use is someone to order the religious gifts we sell. The lady who used to do that has left, and none of us has the time. What would everyone think about letting Jane try her hand at it?"

I am astonished. There is not a single crucifix hanging in my home, my only prayer book is on a shelf in the basement, and my Bible has exactly zero dog-eared pages. My roots are pretty shallow in the forest of religious paraphernalia.

The group talks it over for five minutes before deciding that I probably can't mess it up too badly. They set me loose with six display cabinets full of inventory, a twenty-five thousand dollar yearly budget, and file drawers of catalogs from wholesalers in New York, San Francisco, and Rome. This is one of the major sources of income for the store. I haven't lost my balance yet, but my head begins to spin.

They also show me where the toilet brush is kept.

3

A STREET THEOLOGIAN

She shifts from foot to foot glancing around hopefully at the racks of used clothing in the store. Her medium brown, straight hair is tied back severely in a ponytail, seeming to stretch the worry lines on her forehead and at the corners of her mouth into deeper crevices. She wears no make-up, and she is of the age where makeup helps a great deal.

Our new Society president, Gene, summons me from the back room where I have been sorting and pricing clothing. When we were successful in recruiting his help through a word-of-mouth plea in the parish, and before he had his bearings, we quickly elected him president before he knew what had happened. New at the work, Gene tends to give downtrodden women in need of clothing to the female members.

"She says she needs some clothes," he tells me. "Help her find something—but no fur coats or leather jackets—got it? Write it all down and stick the tally on the filing cabinet."

Not an unusual situation. Although we generally sell the items in our store at rock-bottom prices, even a few dollars can be too much for some of our customers.

Now, as I approach her, I realize she is probably my own age although her last twelve years have pretty obviously not been spent like mine, as suburban mom, part-time teacher, and occasional volunteer. She coughs, and the gravel in her throat hints of too many cigarettes. Her sinewy arms and tightly muscled calves underneath her close-fitting jeans speak plainly of manual labor and all day on her feet and have nothing to do with aerobics classes and long hours spent driving children's carpools. She is a tough lady asking for charity from someone who in other circumstances would be one of her peers. I realize that this is going to be excruciatingly hard for both of us.

"How can I help you?" I inquire as I reach her.

She unexpectedly blushes. "Oh! Not so much—I just got a new job—a good job," she emphasizes. She wedges her hands into the back pockets of her jeans. "It's just that they want me to wear navy blue pants, no jeans, see? I'm waitressing at that new bar on Stadium Drive—nice place. Have you seen it?" I shake my head; my carpool doesn't go through the university campus. "Well, anyway I don't get my first check until next week and the pants are kind of steep at K-Mart and I was hoping . . . I'll pay . . ."

"Sure, no problem," I'm saying as I turn away to lead her to the rack of women's slacks. "What size do you need?"

"I'll pay for them Friday when I get my check." She's not looking at the slacks yet. "I'm not asking you to give them to me, it's just—."

"Don't worry about it," I cut her off again. "What size?"

"Um, eight, sometimes ten." She's still not looking at the pants, only at me.

I pull out a pair of faded Dockers and a wool blend with a plastic belt. "How are these?"

"Great. Perfect. How much are they?"

"Don't worry about it," I repeat casually.

"No, really, I just don't have the money now but I will on Friday."

"Okay," I say and I look at her full in the face for the first time. "But these were donated to us; you are welcome to them. If you want to pay us back, just donate something to the shop when you get a little ahead."

"Oh," she looks relieved, "Sure, I can do that. I've got some stuff I don't need. Good stuff. I'll do that."

"Fine." I feel like apologizing for the awkward way I am dealing with her. It wasn't me who donated the slacks, and I feel like a fraud accepting her gratitude.

Tears are starting to pool in her eyes. "This is really super of you. I didn't know what I was going to do for work tonight. The boss wasn't happy last night when I wore my jeans."

"What else do you need?" Why do I keep interrupting her? "A blouse?"

"No, no, they give us a shirt that has their name on it. I just wash it out every morning."

"Shoes? Socks?"

Her lips tighten and the tears well up again.

"What size?" I turn quickly away from the tears and lead her to the racks of shoes. She picks out a pair of loafers and then we go to the socks. Not much to choose from because those of us who buy socks whenever we need them don't think about donating our old ones. My client finds two pair and looks at me hopefully. I nod and give her a small smile. Next I lead her to the under-wear and the tears come out in full force. I walk over to the cash register and get her a tissue. When she can see well enough to read the sizes on the bras and panties, we are all done in under five minutes. I think of the hours I spend shopping for clothing at the mall and mentally squirm.

I lead her over to the counter and start tallying up her small pile of items as part of our record keeping. While I write, she starts talking. While she talks, God reaches down and touches me.

She's still wiping at her tears as she begins. "I was baptized Catholic as a baby, that's how I knew about you folks. When I was a kid I'd heard St. Vincent de Paul helped people. I can't say I was raised Catholic. My dad, well, he wasn't a very good Catholic . . . or a very good father for that matter," she grimaces. "But anyway, since I grew up, I've gone to one church or another most of the time. My dad doesn't go to church, but he believes in God. There's plenty of folks that go to church but don't believe in God. Matter of fact, not all churches believe in God. Like I said, I've been to quite a few."

I look up from my writing, "How do you know which churches believe in God and which don't?"

She thinks for a moment, "Well, it's like this. At first they all talk about God. 'God loves you, Jesus loves you, we love you'—they all say stuff like that. It's only after you've been in them for a while that you can tell the dif-ference between the ones that really believe what they're saying and the ones that don't."

I'm seriously intrigued. "So? . . . How?"

"After a while some of those places begin to talk about the devil and sins and evil. A little more time and pretty soon that's all they talk about. Ain't long and they give up talking about God altogether. They believe in the devil—they sure do. And I'm not saying they're wrong, but they don't seem to believe in God nearly as much. And they're not nearly as interested in God as they are in the devil either. That's when I know it's time to find me a different church."

I put down my pen and concentrate on her words. She must see that for the first time I am really listening to her because she goes on.

"I'll tell you something else, too; some church people, they talk about forgiving all the time, but they don't have any idea how hard it is to forgive because I don't think they've ever had something really wicked done to them. I've had a hard time with forgiving my dad. I left home when I was fifteen because of him. Most church people, they don't have a clue. Don't get me wrong. Forgiving is the most important thing. If you can't forgive, it eats you up inside. I forgave my dad, and we get along fine now. The rest of my brothers and sisters won't even talk to him."

I realize she's talking about me. I'm one of those people who have only had to forgive little offenses, and I can't even seem to do that properly. "So . . ." I almost don't ask, but then I need to know. "How did you forgive your father?"

She doesn't answer right away. She looks at the other customers and at my colleagues working at the cash register. She takes a couple of steps away from them so that she's talking just to me.

"Well you know how church people say you have to forgive because Jesus forgave the people who crucified him? They say he forgave them while he was hanging on the cross. I heard that over and over. They say if you want to be a Christian, you have to forgive everybody because Jesus did. Well that's not quite right." She pauses, making sure I am not taking offense. "I got my Bible out and I read that story myself—the one about him being crucified. And what actually happened, what he really did say, was: 'Father, forgive them, they don't know what they're doing.' He was talking to God, not to *them*. He was praying for them." She pauses, waiting for me to comprehend.

I stare at her, speechless.

She smiles, "That's right, too; you can look it up."

"You—You're right."

"What good does it do to forgive people who are laughing at you and are still in the middle of killing you? They don't *want* forgiveness for one thing. For Chrisakes, he still had the damn nails in his hands! God didn't ask *that* much of him. And I don't believe he asks that much of us either. So that's how I forgave my dad. I did what Jesus did. I prayed, 'God, *you forgive him*, because right now I can't. Those old nails were still in my hands and God understood that. I prayed that way for a long, long time. And one day when I didn't feel them quite so much, I could forgive. I'm the only one in my family who will go see my dad."

I bag up her clothing. As I hand it to her, she thanks me again and turns to walk out of the store. I ask her a question to keep her from leaving. Then I follow her to the door, hoping for still more of her amazing insights. When we are out on the sidewalk, she reaches into her blouse and pulls a pack of cigarettes out of her bra. She lights up and inhales deeply, with a sigh. And then comes my moment of ultimate spiritual humility. She asks shyly, "Will you pray for me?"

"Yes," I answer, "Yes, of course." And then, from deep down I say, "And will you pray for me?"

She looks at me shrewdly, hesitating. "You don't look like you need it," she observes matter-of-factly.

It takes my breath away.

"Oh, yes—I do. Please, will you?"

"OK," she agrees, and then she smiles.

Ten minutes later, insisting that she really does have to get to work, I reluctantly let her detach herself from me, and I wander slowly back into the store. Virginia and Dorothy cluck their tongues in sympathy and say to me, "My, that was nice of you to listen to that poor woman go on and on. Sometimes they just want to talk, don't they?"

"No, no, that wasn't it at all," I protest. "Honestly, I wish I hadn't interrupted her so much. I should have let her talk more."

They smile fondly at me. "You certainly have a lot of patience, Jane."

4

REINFORCEMENTS

It is spring. Summer approaches and St. Vincent de Paul experiences the uncharacteristic addition of two new volunteers. Jim and Bonnie are a recently retired couple from the parish and, aside from a winter home in Arizona that beckons them occasionally, they are willing to enlist. We take a leap of faith at our next meeting and decide to stay open instead of closing down for the months of June, July and August, as has been the custom. But as we begin to divide up the three six-hour days per week that the store will be open, our enthusiasm dips. We all have vacation plans, some of our regulars play golf weekly, and my two grade school-age daughters will be home from school.

I know that my venerable fellow volunteers need a break, but I'm also sure my kids have better ideas for warm days than spending them in a stuffy store. What we really need is a system of conscription, but there is nothing in the St. Vincent de Paul manual about how to set that up.

"Tell the bishop to find us some helpers," orders one of the two Bernies at our next monthly meeting. "We're doing important work and he should pound the pulpit and get some people in here."

Everyone nods in agreement, but I seriously doubt that this is going to happen. The bishop has many crises to deal with, and our lack of volunteers is surely not one of them. "We could put an ad in the church bulletin," I suggest reasonably.

"That never works." They shoot that down along with my next three suggestions, all of which they dismiss with a wave of their arthritic hands. An open house is too much work, the parish volunteer fair takes place in the fall, and a "volunteers wanted" sign in the window could attract God-knows-who. It begins to dawn on me that what my comrades really want is for me to personally recruit some people and to do it fast.

"High school kids?" I suggest.

"Not reliable."

"Young mothers with small children in tow?"

"Impossible. Where would we put babies and toddlers?"

"Recent retirees?

"They're all traveling and golfing."

"But who else is there?" I ask.

"What we need," says Bernie number two, "is five or six women in their thirties or forties, who don't have jobs and whose children are old enough to leave home alone for six hours twice a week." They all nod in unison and look at me expectantly.

The incredible part is that they mean it.

They are picturing themselves forty years ago. They are remembering an era of single-income families with children closely spaced whose only extracurricular activities involved a wooden bat, a ball, and an empty lot two blocks from home.

"Well, good luck with that," I murmur.

"I'll call the bishop," Bernie number one says.

Meanwhile, the donated clothing and household items in our backroom are mushrooming into tottering piles up to the rafters. Bulging cardboard boxes and plastic garbage bags line the ramp to the back door at waist height. The people who donate are generous to a fault and almost apologetic when they see how buried we are in their gifts.

One lady stares wide-eyed at the sagging shelves and narrow aisles when she drops off a trunkload of clothing. While I fill out a donation receipt for her, she says, "I'm so grateful that you'll take this stuff. It's my mother's, and she would only let me clean it out of her house on the condition that it went to charity. I know some of it isn't usable, but she was helping me pack the boxes and she wouldn't let me throw any of it away." She extracts a twenty-dollar bill from her purse. "Mark this down as part of the donation. It's for taking all of this off my hands. God bless you."

This lady is a good reminder to me that, if you put it in context, junk is not junk.

This avalanche of nonjunk is not unusual; we take the bad with the good, or we wouldn't get any good things at all. Still, we have our limits.

The next gentleman pulls up in a BMW and wants to give us a computer.

"Does it work?" I ask. I have learned to ask this.

"Perfectly. It only needs a hard drive. I removed it because it had some sensitive material on it."

I explain to him that we are not equipped to replace hard drives in old computers.

"Well, what am I supposed to do with it?" He demands.

I shrug and point to our dumpster. "You're welcome to use that if you want."

He is affronted but insists that we will be able to sell the computer as is. I watch him unload it and he wedges it onto our workbench. It makes him feel better, but we both know that after he drives away I will lug it to the dumpster.

There is a type of desperation in our overabundance. It's similar to a flood in the same way that water, the source of life, when excessively present, can suffocate the life right out of you. I can see on the next donor's face that she suspects that we are not overjoyed to receive the tag ends of her garage sale.

Yet sometimes we undervalue a donation. It's oddly disappointing when antique dealers buy something off of our shelves because it can only mean that we priced it too low. Since every penny we make goes to the poor, we like to get a fair price.

While I'm disposing of the computer, Jim hollers to me from the door and asks if I will take a look at the latest drop-off.

"It's in a wooden crate," he tells me, "that says *Black Label Scotch, Glasgow* on the side of it. It's a bunch of Catholic missals still in their original boxes. They're kind of old, but maybe someone will be interested in them for the nostalgia of the Latin."

Jim and I go to the backroom to check out the treasure and spot it near the door. Jim picks up the entire box and sets it on the workbench so we can look over the contents. Sure enough, more than a dozen unopened pre-Vatican II Sunday missals.

"Are they worth anything?" Jim asks me.

"Hmm . . . not sure. But several of our regular customers collect old religious books. Someone will want them." I pause and peer at the side of the crate. "Ever hear of *Black Label Scotch*?"

He shrugs noncommittally. "What price shall I put on the missals?"

"First, let's see what kind of shape they're in." I reach into the crate and pull out a red- and-white printed book box. Blowing the dust away, I pry open the top flap.

Bugs come crawling out.

Hundreds of them. Bookworms. All over my hands, on my shoes, wriggling across the floor—ugh!

Jim says that he wishes I would be more mature about it.

Eventually I am.

Anyway, the conclusion is that we throw a dozen books containing Holy Scripture into the dumpster and sell the scotch crate for ten dollars.

Working for God can be a strange business.

After some liberal use of bug spray, I go back to throwing shoes into a pile under the winter coat racks. The idea is that I will get around to pricing them later, but for now I will sort the keepers from the dogs and get on with it.

While I am tossing shoes, a young man comes in looking for a free coat and shoes.

This is not an unusual request—it happens daily—but this time I am puzzled. The man is wearing what looks like a brand new coat, and his shoes might be unstylish but they are shiny and scuff free. When he sees the skepticism on my face, he explains his dilemma.

He has recently been released from the penitentiary. All the clothes he is wearing were given to him as a government farewell. Understandably, he doesn't want to apply for jobs wearing the easily recognized prison-issue brown shoes and coat.

My mind is whirling with the hundreds of reasons he might have spent time in prison and the fact that two seventy-something volunteers and I are all that's keeping him from pulling out a weapon, taking what he wants, and walking out the door. But I force myself to clamp down on my whirly thoughts, and I look at him again.

He is standing in front of me empty-handed, self-consciously embarrassed, with a hopeful look on his face. His hair is brushed, his face clean shaven, and his only visible tattoos are the decorative kind. The man has done his time. He only wants a different image to show the world, and he hopes we can help provide him with one.

I can't think of why not.

As quickly as possible I find him a used coat in exchange for his brand new one. The release of the tell-tale apparel obviously relieves him of a burden. He is grateful and polite, and I begin to relax a little bit. I can't find any shoes, however, because the pile I have been making has reached swamplike conditions: a multicolored morass of tangled laces, lolling tongues, and upturned soles. He helps me search for a while, but eventually he gives up and leaves.

So I sort shoes for three hours. My back aches, my fingers turn black, and no one has to tell me it is my own doing. By the end of the day the shoes are all paired, sized, priced, and lined up neatly on wooden shelves. As I sort and price, I find myself thinking and praying for the ex-con. He is the first person I have ever met who has done time in prison. Strangely, now that the shoes are in order, I find myself hoping that he will come back and find what he needs.

I am also now praying hourly for two new volunteers to fill the vacancies on our staff. This shortage has gone beyond serious. Two of our long-time volunteers have reached an age where they feel they can't be relied upon to come in every week. Replacing two white-haired champions is not an easy task. As I pray for some "new" old ladies, I realize that my prayer life has never been so strong.

Meanwhile, I have been doing some reading and gradually find myself charmed by the whole idea of the St. Vincent de Paul Society the same way that Dorothy charmed me on that first day I walked into the store.

Frédéric Ozanam and his friends, a bunch of Parisian college students, formed the St. Vincent de Paul Society about 170 years ago. In the midst of a deceptively harmless Bible study, it dawned on them that Jesus spent inordinate amounts of time helping poor people.

Maybe he was dropping a clue?

They launched themselves into the neighborhood, helped wherever they found a need for it, and proceeded to age in place.

It explains our present St. Vincent de Paul scenario of old folks battling almost solo against the misery of poverty, and it also gives me a notion about recapturing some of the original vigor of the organization.

The idea of college students intrigues me. It just might be possible that this challenge of finding and training reinforcements for the summer can be easily remedied on the local college campuses, of which there are two within walking distance of the store. Over 25,000 strong, half-educated young people with few signs of arthritis living in the neighborhood—how perfect can it be?

Enter a couple of young men who have hauled heavy furniture occasionally for us in the past. On a Saturday morning in late spring, I meet Dan and Patrick in the parking lot as they unload a sofa-sleeper from the back of a pickup truck. They are graduates of the local Catholic high school, which is how they found themselves on our call list of strong muscles for occasional furniture moving.

How to entice them to be more regular in their altruism? Remembering Dorothy's lesson, I remind myself that there's nothing like asking. My first few pitches are strikes, but eventually we connect.

Would they like to learn how to run the cash register?

"Not really the best use of our talents."

Would they be interested in supervising the intake of donations?

"We're not seeing that at all."

Would they like to act as our store guards on Friday afternoons? Just for a month or so?

They mull it over. "This is gonna cost extra."

"We'll double your pay."

"Bonus! Wait. Aren't we volunteers?"

"You're a lot more than just volunteers. It will be your job to fit all the non-working electronic equipment into our dumpster."

"Now we're talking."

Tentatively, I lend them a sledgehammer and allow them to reduce a non-functional eight-track player to shards. They are ready. Are we?

It's not long before our store guards become full members—running the cash register, interviewing clients, sorting and tagging donations, and joining the prayer group.

As the springtime wanes, I ponder how to harness their energy, enthusiasm, and humor for the approaching summer. What catches me by surprise is their reluctance to leave.

"We've heard that the store is closed on Fridays during the summer. And why's that?"

"Volunteers need a break," I explain.

They become unnaturally serious. "If we get enough people to keep the store open, would you let us?"

"Well . . . yeah, sure, but . . . why would you do that?"

Here is their answer: "Dude, you don't know how much this place means to us."

So I give them a store key and take the summer off to spend time with my daughters. Every other week I stop by to check how they are doing. They have recruited two coeds to assist at the cash register and one of their brothers. It looks like a full and happy crew to me, and I enjoy my summer guilt free.

On one of my checking-on-the-boys days, as I park in the lot, a patrol car pulls up next to my car. The driver's window rolls down, and the officer says to me, "Is this St. Vincent de Paul?"

I agree that it is and he asks, "Do you throw computers into your dumpster?"

Uh oh. Good old Catholic guilt nearly has me blubbering a confession, but I hedge. "Is that a bad thing?"

The policeman exchanges a look with his partner. "We picked up a couple of guys pushing a grocery cart full of computer equipment. They described this place to us and swore that they got all the stuff out of the dumpster. Could that be possible?"

"Their story has an excellent chance of being true, Officer."

He rolls his eyes and gives me the name of a place that recycles computer parts.

That works for me.

Near the end of August, one of our college students, Joe, asks me, "Did it bother you that we took over the store?"

"No, not at all," I answer truthfully. "We needed to make room, or you never would have learned what you could do."

"Hmm . . . yeah, that makes sense actually." He nods. "Lookin' good, lookin' good."

The summer ends, and our college students transfer toward their future lives. I am very sorry to see them go, but I never expected them to be more than a stopgap. My daughters return to school, and I am back on the Friday schedule as the key holder.

On the first day that we are short of help, two people walk into the shop and offer their services: a young mother whose kids have just started back to school, and a fortyish ex-policeman who runs his own security consulting firm. It takes me a moment before I realize that these are the replacement "old ladies" we have been praying for.

"How did you find out that we needed help?" I ask them.

"The bishop sent me," the man says.

5

HOME VISITS

Let us go to the Poor.

—BLESSED FRÉDÉRIC OZANAM, FOUNDER OF
THE SOCIETY OF ST. VINCENT DE PAUL

Beds are hard to come by. People give away fur coats more often than they donate beds. At our store, the bed shortage translates into five or more yellow sticky notes on the bulletin board scrawled with someone's telephone number and the triple underlined phrase, "Call if we get a bed."

There is a bed dealer who on a weekly basis comes through the store. He saunters through the sorting room, up the ramp, and into our furniture storage area to check on the merchandise. If we happen to have a bed, he always tries to haggle down the price, but we don't bargain with him because we know that he intends to sell the bed for a profit to someone else. We don't like it when this dealer buys beds, which are precious and few in supply, but on the other hand, he pays in cash. Now that we are spending down the bank balance, we have to think about our clients who need money to keep the heat on more than they need beds to sleep on. Occasionally we will sell to the dealer if none of the people on the sticky notes answers our calls.

It's early morning, and I'm working up front at the cash register. A call comes in, and Dorothy answers it. The woman on the other end asks to speak to "whoever is in charge." We are short-handed so Dorothy decides that the person in charge is either her or me. She picks me and hands over the phone.

On the line is a nurse at the local hospital, and she has a problem. They are preparing to release a woman patient the next day who has been hospitalized for over a month, but the lady has no bed.

I start to tell her that we don't have any beds either, but the nurse interrupts. "We have a bed to give her, but we don't have any way to pick it up or deliver it to her house. Do you people help with that sort of thing?"

Well, the simple answer is "no" because that particular request has not been tried on us before. The more complicated answer is "yes," because the St. Vincent de Paul Society is pledged to help the poor in whatever way we are able.

"*Maybe*," I say.

"The bed is at my grandmother's house," continues the nurse. "She moved into a senior-care facility, and we sold her house. The realtor has already hired a furniture dealer to come clean out the place and haul everything away because we need to have the house empty today for the new owners. But if you can get over there before two o'clock, the realtor says she'll save the bed for us."

"Let me get back with you on that."

First obstacle to bed rescue: there are only two of us running the shop, and Dorothy is so tiny and frail I wouldn't ask her to lift a footstool let alone a bed. And even if I go to fetch the bed, Dorothy can't run the store by herself. I call my sister who works in the office of one of the local Catholic grade schools and invite her to take her lunch break while running our cash register. She is okay with that.

Second obstacle: no way can I carry a bed by myself let alone load it into my truck. Dorothy suggests I call our president, Gene, who keeps trying to retire from the work. Gene is only eighty years old, and Dorothy thinks he needs to get over this silly idea that he's too old for volunteering.

"He's bigger than you," she tells me. "Between the two of you, it shouldn't be a problem."

"Um . . . yeah. I'm going to have to take your word on that." But, in the middle of a Friday morning, my options are limited so I call Gene and after some achy bone-felt sighs, he agrees to help.

I call the nurse back and "Operation bed rescue" is underway.

Gene and I drive across town and find the realtor holding off the furniture dealer. She points to the last bedroom on the right and says to take everything in the room that we want. We find a single bed with a nearly new mattress and box spring, a two-drawer bedside table complete with a reading lamp, and a small bookshelf. It's a lovely, grandmotherly sort of place with flowered comforters, fluffy pillows, and solid maple furniture painted a creamy white. The realtor tells us to take the sheets and bedding too, so Gene and I quickly stuff it all into garbage bags and carry it out of the house.

Gene is jumping on and off the tailgate of my truck like a sixteen-year-old, so I tell him to cut it out because he's making me look bad.

"Are we going to deliver this today?" he asks.

He looks mildly disappointed when I tell him that our patient/client won't be released from the hospital until tomorrow, which is Saturday, and that my husband, Dean, will more than likely be helping me deliver it. Dean doesn't know this yet.

I pull out the address of the woman's home, and it has one of those fractional house numbers that tells me the place is likely an upstairs apartment in a converted older home. Even though I've lived in Kalamazoo my entire life, I don't recognize the name of the street. Gene looks at it and shakes his head, "Good luck going into that neighborhood," he says.

The next day Dean and I and his friend Dave drive up to the saddest house on the roughest street in the worst neighborhood in town. An unmarked, windowless van is idling across the street with several young men leaning into the open rear doors. They look over their shoulders at our overloaded pickup truck and quickly shut their van and lean nonchalantly on the closed doors, watching us.

Dean and Dave exchange raised eyebrows, and my husband says to me, "Stay in the truck."

He and Dave get out and walk up and knock on the front door of the house. A shirtless young man opens it and slowly looks over the two middle-aged white guys standing on his porch steps. I don't hear the conversation, but after some gesturing by the young man I get the idea that we should drive around to the back of the house. Dean and Dave hop back in beside me and begin pulling the truck into the narrow driveway that takes up the entire width of space between the house and the one next door.

Abruptly, the side door of the house opens and something small and black clatters across the driveway in front of the truck. Dean brakes and stops so as not to run over whatever it was that landed in front of the tires just as the same shirtless young man pops his head out the door and waves an unnecessary hand to halt our progress. He leaps down the two steps and dashes out in front of the bumper to retrieve a cell phone.

Holding it up, smiling, he calls out to us, "Slipped out of my hand," and shrugs innocently before returning into the house and slamming the door.

I wonder out loud, "How could his cell phone go flying out the door like that?"

Dave grins and asks me, "You think maybe he intended us to run over it?"

"But why would—" I stop. "Oh . . . that's very strange. . . ."

Dave says to Dean, "Did you notice that his pupils were dilated?"

Dean laughs and says to me, "I think I'm going to like this new volunteer job of yours, Sweetie."

Around the back of the house, the small yard is gravel surrounded by overgrown honeysuckle bushes. The paint color on the siding is inconsistent front to back and up and down. There is a two-story back porch with an enclosed staircase leading up to the second-floor apartment. While Dean and Dave begin unloading the furniture, I knock on the door at the bottom of the stairs. I notice that the door has received repeated battering around the lockset and the dented kick plate might have been useful once or twice. It seems silly to think that anyone in the overhead apartment could possibly hear my rapping, but I try twice more before grasping the knob and finding it locked.

The guys have the furniture standing in the gravel by now so they tell me to wait with it while they walk around to the front to inquire if the fellow with the slippery cell phone has a way to alert his upstairs neighbor of our arrival.

He does.

He walks into the driveway, cups his hands around his mouth and hollers at the upstairs window, "Anita! Yo, Anita! Your bed is here!"

Twenty seconds later, a hand pushes up the double-hung casement, and Anita sticks her head out. "My what's here?"

I wave my hand cheerfully and call up to her, "We've brought you a bed. Can we bring it up for you?"

She stretches the entire upper half of her body out now and gapes down at us and our truck and the furniture piled beside it as if we just dropped out of the sky. "Who are you?"

I wince. This is going to sound too weird, even to my ears, but I call it out in front of the whole neighborhood anyway. "We're the Saint Vincent de Paul Society, and we've got a bed for you. Do you want it?"

Her neighbor says helpfully, "You all can just leave it here, and I'll help her get it up there."

Anita cusses him out and tells us to meet her at the back door.

It takes several up and down trips to get the mattress, the box spring, the frame, the headboard, the bookcase and the side table into her apartment. While we do this, the neighbor slips past us into Anita's home and gathers up an armload of items he says he left there by mistake. Anita, dressed in a nightgown and looking as healthy as someone might be expected to look after spending a month in the hospital, is fussing at him to clear out as he dashes from living room to kitchen to bedroom collecting his things.

As we reconstruct the bed in a gray-carpeted, gray-painted bedroom that holds exactly five overflowing ashtrays and an ironing board, another unhelpful neighbor appears in the apartment. Anita releases a double measure of arm waving and protests at their continued scurrying about her kitchen. Eventually they find everything they are looking for and they depart.

There is a sofa that is very much in the way on account of it standing on end in the small hallway leading from the kitchen into the bedroom. Dean asks Anita if it is something we could move for her.

She looks weary after the battle with her neighbors. "I'd be grateful if you could just put it out on the curb for me. It's all broken up. Those people don't respect nobody's stuff. They've been using my place to do all their badness while I'm lying in the hospital and can't do nothing about it. They ate all my food and they left their trash and their cigarettes all over the place. If I don't keep my door locked all the time, they run in and out like they live here."

I hear this as I am carrying the bedding through the door. She leans heavily against the kitchen counter and her anger slowly fades into confusion as she spots the flowers and ruffles. "Who did you people say you are?"

My arms are loaded to overflowing, but I stop and try again to explain who we represent, but "Saint Vincent de Paul" isn't a name that means anything to her. I look around the disordered kitchen. There is no food in sight and oddly, no food smells, either. There aren't any dirty dishes on the counters or in the sink, but everything is thick with ash and dust. In the general clutter of discarded scraps of paper, I see small twisted pieces of wire and the occasional old clothes. It's like a house where people live and sleep but no one eats.

I ask, "Do you have some friends who can look after you while you're recovering?"

"I ain't got any friends."

I stop. I have never heard someone older than sixteen say this. Anita looks to be closer to forty.

In denial, I start to argue with her, "Family? Do you belong to a church? Are there any neighbors . . .?"

She scowls and gestures at her trash-strewn floor. "You think I left my place looking like this? All my so-called friends and neighbors made this mess." She reaches down her hand and pulls up the hem of her nightgown to reveal a diaper-size bandage covering her left thigh. "I got this infection that the doctors worked on for over a month. They almost amputated my leg but I begged them not to because how am I gonna live with only one leg? They saved it in the end, but they took out huge chunks before they was all done cleaning it up." Anita shakes her head and drapes the gown back over the ghastly wound. "I ain't got no friends and don't want any."

In the awkward silence I say softly, "Well, the nurses at the hospital must have taken a shine to you, or they wouldn't have gone to all the trouble of getting a bed."

The bitterness on her face fades to disbelief. "The nurses gave it to me?"

I nod and explain in the quiet of the dusty kitchen how it came about that we are there. While we talk, Dean and Dave finish removing the broken sofa and setting up the bed. They come out and ask Anita if there is anything else she would like carried to the curb, and she leads them into the living room to point out a tattered lounger and the bare mattress in the middle of the floor that she has been using as a bed. While they work, I carry the bedding into the little bedroom and spread and tuck ruffles and flowers liberally over the mattress. I plug in the lamp and set it on the bedside table and put a hot water bottle in the drawer. I find an old rag and scoop up all the ashtrays and dump them in a wastebasket in the kitchen. The ironing board gets folded and stashed in the empty closet, and then I do a quick once-over picking up papers and dust bunnies from the gray carpet.

Just as I finish transforming the place from a Kansas twister into the Land of Oz, Anita shuffles back in and gasps. She sits slowly down on the grandma bed and smoothes the bedspread with her palm. "It's beautiful," she whispers.

"Yes," I agree. Dean and Dave appear in the doorway and nod their heads in satisfaction.

"The nurses gave me this?"

"Yes, they wanted you to have it." I ask if there is some medicine we can pick up for her at a pharmacy.

"Visiting nurses are supposed to come every day to change the bandages," she tells us as she climbs between the sheets. There are tears in her eyes. "In my whole life I've never had my own bed before."

That does it. We all get tears. I ask if there is anything else we can do.

"Could you lock the door when you let yourselves out?"

I write down our store address and phone number and leave it on the bedside table and tell her to call us if she needs anything.

"Just a bed, that's all I needed," she says as I pull the comforter over her shoulders. "I am so blessed," she says. "God is so good."

6

WILLING TO BE
DISTURBED

The first thing that I discover as a new member of the St. Vincent de Paul Society is that if I want to help the poor and expect to be thanked for it, then I am working for the wrong charity.

Everyone in the group is a volunteer. We have no executive director, no volunteer coordinator, and no recognition dinner at the end of the year. We do have an elected president, a vice-president, and a secretary, each of whom carry the responsibility of filling out and archiving the mountain of paperwork involved in running a nonprofit. These additional burdens are considerable, and no one expects the officers to stand at the door at closing time to shake our hands in gratitude as we leave for the day.

What's more, the people we help are not usually having the best day of their lives when we meet them. They walk through our door seeking assistance with an eviction notice, a utility shut-off, or a prescription medicine they can't afford, and they are more likely to be angry at the situation they find themselves in rather than bursting with gratitude.

Saint Vincent de Paul himself understood well the loss of dignity that needy people suffer, and he admonished his followers like this:

"Don't make the poor ask for what God, their Father, wants them to have. We should apologize if they have to ask for what they need."

The gentleman is blue collar, anxious, obviously unused to asking for help. He questions me quietly so that no one else in the store will overhear.

"Do you give clothes to people who need them? It's not for me, it's for my cousin."

"Your cousin has to come down and ask for himself," I tell him.

"He works five in the morning until seven. He just got the job and can't miss, but he only has one pair of pants."

I must look a little skeptical at this claim.

He hesitates but then explains. "He just got out of prison. It was his second time." A shrug. "Anyway, I told his parole officer that he could live with me until he got on his feet. He's family; if I don't give him a chance, who will? They taught him to hang drywall in there. This is the first decent job he's ever had, but he doesn't get paid until next Friday. I gave him some of my pants but he's six foot three and skinny as a rail. No way he can fit in my stuff. You know anything about drywall? The dust? His pants stand up by themselves when he takes them off. There's no time to wash and dry them."

On the clothes racks we find sweatpants, shirts, socks, and a winter coat. As I bag the clothes, he asks, "Can I rake your leaves? I'd like to do something to help you folks out. I'll make sure my cousin comes in to thank you when he gets a day off, but let me do something today."

I tell him it isn't necessary, but he asks again, and then another time after I hand him the bag. I refuse again just as my coworker Jim walks by us.

Jim, overhearing the offer, is more perceptive than I. "I'll get you a rake," he tells him. "Thanks very much, it would be a great help."

The man rakes every leaf into a tidy pile. When he comes back inside, he is no longer anxious or uneasy. He shakes our hands, gathers up his small bag of clothing and walks out.

This man raking the leaves at the St. Vinnie's thrift shop is confirmation of a niggling suspicion I have about the place. Gradually, over the first few months that I work there, it starts to become uneasily clear to me that we are not trying to change the world. We aren't trying to change poor people either.

The only thing it seems we are trying to change is ourselves.

This does not sit well with me. It is not enough. I am programmed to change the world. Changing myself seems pathetic in comparison.

What's more: I am beginning to suspect that this is not something that can be done with bumper stickers.

One morning, during our prayer time at the store, we are reading the teachings of St. Vincent, and the saint's instructions are clear:

"The poor are our masters; they are our kings; we must obey them. It is no exaggeration to call them this, since our Lord is in the poor."

After a brief silence while we ponder these words, one of our Bernies lifts her head and complains to the rest of us, "That sure seems backwards to me."

I nod in sympathy with her. Helping the poor makes sense to me, obeying them does not. Then I remember how my master wanted to rake the leaves and I refused.

My masters have much to teach me.

The next time I walk into the store, bread is everywhere. Half a dozen thirty-gallon sacks of it fill up the floor space of the clothes-sorting room.

"But we don't do bread," I say to our latest recruits, Pat and Mary Kay, as we stare at the deliciously adorned floor.

Pat stoops over and pulls open one of the bags to reveal bagels, brioches, buns, and bread sticks. "It's one of those miracles again," she sighs.

Mary Kay reaches down and plucks out a cherry Danish. "Where's the fish?"

I look at her doubtfully. "More likely it's a donation from someone who thought we had a food pantry here. What are we going to do with it?"

No one knows. We shrug our shoulders at each other, step over the sacks, and wait for a sign from heaven that is more specific. Sometimes we are so "apostle-esque."

Around noon, Walter, our newest volunteer with "organizational skills," walks into the store and explains the parable. "Give it away," he says. "We got this great opportunity to be the distributor of a bakery's day-old bread. I figured we could just let our customers and clients take what they want."

This is a fine idea of course, but lacking any suitable place to store it overnight, we only have about three hours left in the day to give away about fifty pounds of baked goods. Pat, Mary Kay, and I very quickly turn into pushers.

"Would you like some bread to go with that sweater you're buying?"

"Have you ever considered bagels for supper?"

People are mostly delighted to help us with our dilemma. They try their best to think of neighbors and friends who might want it, and they haul away grocery sacks of the stuff.

Late in the afternoon, one customer, an elderly lady, looks over the arrangement of sacks in the sorting room and says to me, "I'm not so hungry that I would eat bread off the floor. Thank you, but no thank you."

I am embarrassed.

She is right of course. And she is my teacher. Charity does not excuse treating people without dignity.

After she leaves, we gather up the sacks from the floor, place them on our sorting tables, and make available a package of napkins so people don't have to use their bare hands.

Fifteen minutes before closing we still have enough bread to fill "twelve large baskets*" so to speak. The last customer of the day selects a couple dozen bagels, and it looks like we are going to have to throw the rest into the dumpster.

---

*In the Gospel stories, there were twelve baskets of food left over after Jesus miraculously fed thousands of people.

"Don't be shy," I urge the woman.

"You want me to take more?" she asks.

"As much as you can, we close at three and don't know what to do with it."

She looks thoughtful. "I work in a group home. They would love this. I could put it in their freezer."

We fill the trunk of her car.

Pat waves cheerfully as the woman drives away and asks me, "In a time before freezers, what do you suppose the apostles did with those twelve baskets of bread?"

"Thank God we didn't get the fish, too," says Mary Kay.

7

SAINTS AND SINNERS

September 27 is the feast day of St. Vincent de Paul and therefore, by association, it is also the feast day of the St. Vincent de Paul Society.

Now that I spend large quantities of my time pouring over religious gift catalogs, meeting with salesmen, and waiting on customers, the saints have started to become something like a large extended family for me. I'm actually beginning to think of them as people.

I come to the store on our feast day and find a sticky note attached to the computer screen. My colleagues use the donated computer as a sort of bulletin board that doesn't need pins. They leave all their notes for me stuck to it. This one says "Jane, we're out of St. Gerard holy cards again."

This is puzzling because I have restocked St. Gerard twice in the space of two months. I wonder out loud, "What's this fascination with St. Gerard?"

Virginia, our cashier, explains. "He's the patron saint of expectant mothers and troubled pregnancies. We always need his cards. Order a bunch next time."

Overhearing our conversation, one of our customers nods. "My father is Gerard. He was born when his parents were forty-five years old."

Her companion looks thoughtful. "Hmm . . . my brother's middle name is Gerard. I've never thought about why they named him that."

I've been introduced to many saints this way over the past few months and—new for me—I have even taken to wearing a Miraculous medal* around my neck. We sell so many of them that I figure there must be something to the stories about it. Because our shop is two blocks from the regional cancer treatment center, I've learned to keep St. Peregrine's prayer cards on hand too. St. Christopher medals are our biggest sellers, and they go especially well on visor clips for cars. Soon-to-be-deployed soldiers want St. Michael, musicians love Cecilia, actors seek out Genesius, and hunters come in for Hubert.

I've had to catch on fast. There are still times when I get caught unprepared for a rush on a particular saint, but that's not going to happen this September 27. I have ordered a box of fifty paper holy cards with St. Vincent's picture on the front and a prayer on the back. We are planning to celebrate by giving them away to our customers.

As the morning goes on, we slip one into each shopping bag like a promotional flyer, adding a brief mention of our feast day. Most people are too polite to refuse even if they don't have a clue what a patron saint is or what the

---

*A Miraculous medal is a medal bearing an image of the Blessed Virgin Mary, which many Catholics wear as a sign of faith and in hope of special graces through Mary's intercession.

purpose of a holy card could be. They smile and thank us and leave quickly. Catholics will never win prizes as evangelizers.

The phone rings. I answer it with our usual greeting; "St. Vincent de Paul, may I help you?"

"Um . . . yes. May I speak to Vincent, please?"

This is clearly a telemarketer with a limited knowledge of Catholicism, but we are too busy at the moment for me to explain two thousand years of dead holy people.

I answer truthfully, "I'm afraid that he is deceased."

"Oh. Are you his wife?"

Now I'm working hard not to laugh. "No. No, I'm not. She's not here either."

"I'll call back next week and try to speak to Mrs. De Paul then."

"That will be fine," I tell him and he hangs up. Obviously, I need help with promoting this saint thing.

As I turn away from the phone, a middle-aged couple walks into the store and hands me a ten-dollar bill. I thank them, of course, give them a holy card, and ask what's up.

The gentleman answers, "We went to Mass this morning, and the sermon was about St. Vincent de Paul. The priest mentioned where your shop was located, so on our way out of town we thought we would stop and make a donation to your work. We live in North Carolina, and we're visiting our daughter this week and are just about to head home."

The couple leaves, and Dorothy and I look at each other in amazement.

"What should we do with it?" Dorothy asks. "Put it in the cash register?"

"Don't do that," I say. "It will only mess up the balance sheet. Leave it behind the counter and we'll figure something out at the end of the day."

Not ten minutes later, a man walks in the same door and asks if we can help him with money for gas for his car. He has a long involved story ready, but we hand over the ten dollars before he has finished telling it. He is a bit befuddled by our lack of suspicion, but we rapidly explain about St. Vincent's feast and pile a holy card on top of the money in his palm.

"Pass it on to someone else when you get the chance," Dorothy tells him.

"Pass it on? Yeah, okay. I'll do that. Thanks, thanks very much." And he's gone.

"Wow," I say. "That was fast. Usually it's not so obvious what the Man upstairs wants us to do with his money."

"Easy come, easy go," Dorothy says.

September passes quickly and then October. One crisp, cold morning I arrive at the store just in time to see a furnace company van pull up next to the building. This is not a good sign. We have applied ourselves conscientiously to giving away the money in the bank account, leaving a small reserve in case of emergencies. Furnace trouble could take care of that surplus in short order.

As I open the door to my car, a young man in work overalls climbs out of the van. "Do we have problems?" I ask him.

"I don't know about you," he says, "but I sure do. What's the most powerful prayer a person can say? It feels like I'm fighting evil itself."

Raw desperation can be startling.

It takes me a moment to take in what he is saying. He looks to be in his midtwenties, clean shaven, with tidy fingernails and round ears, and no signs of tattoos or jewelry hanging in unusual places. He's just an ordinary furnace repair technician as far as I can see. Why would old Satan pick on somebody like him? But it's not my job to decide that, I remind myself. It's my job to help people in need. Hoo-boy, what have I gotten myself into now?

"Umm . . ." I think rapidly through my newly gained grasp of prayers and saints. "I guess what you need is St. Michael on your side."

Recognition shows on his face. "Michael the Archangel? Guy with a sword and armor?" He nods to himself. "Sounds like a plan."

We begin walking toward the front door, and I ask him, "Do you want a prayer card or a medal?"

"Better give me both."

We get through Halloween with no further movement from the dark side.

In fact, we sell more merchandise for this pagan holiday than we do for some Christian ones. The college students especially like our collection of "vintage" clothing. They point and giggle while looking through the women's dress rack and buy dozens of our men's ties.

Many of the neighborhood moms and grandmas pull pouting youngsters into the shop in hopes of piecing together odds and ends for a costume. We are ready for this and have put together a large display of unique items ranging from cheap jewelry to tuxedos, along with used costumes that have been donated. Usually both kids and adults leave happy.

I bring my own daughters downtown one Saturday, and they have a grand time figuring out what to wear among the racks. They choose elbow-length gloves, sparkly pumps, and prom gowns, and it doesn't even bruise my budget. After the holiday my eldest, who is a precocious economics student, sells her costume to one of her friend's parents for a profit.

Hmm. I had secretly hoped that my volunteering for a charity would have an influence on my girls.

Shortly after we have stored away the sparkly shoes and funny hats, I find myself interviewing a young woman who is asking for assistance with an overdue utility bill. She tells me she is all alone in the world; both parents deceased, no siblings, no grandparents, no aunts, uncles, or cousins.

This is unfathomable.

I am the sixth of eight children and have so many relatives that we rent out the church gym for Thanksgiving dinner. Plus, as I have been learning lately, I have centuries of saints on my side, not to mention all my friends and relatives who have passed on before me. What must it be like to feel all alone in the world?

The young woman is twenty-two, she works full time in a nursing home and has continued to live in the apartment that she and her mother shared. Her finances have steadily worsened since her mother's death two years ago. Due to the loss of her mother's income and financial advice, and because of the lack of relatives, she is reduced to going around to churches for help even though she doesn't belong to one herself.

"Do you talk to your mom?" I ask as I fill out the paperwork to help her.

She looks startled, and then her face flushes a deep red. She peers at me closely to see if I am serious. "Sometimes . . . sometimes I do talk to her." She pauses. "Do you think that's crazy?"

"No. I talk to my Dad and he's been dead several years."

Her eyes widen. "Actually, I talk to my mom every-day. I can't help it, I miss her a lot."

I nod calmly and continue with the paperwork. "Do you know that she can still pray for you, just like when she was alive?"

"No one ever told me that."

"Well, now you know." I give her a promissory note for help with her electric bill. "Next time you talk to your mom, ask for her prayers. She's a little closer to Jesus than we are. It's bound to help."

"Thank you," she says, shaking my hand with more enthusiasm than the promissory note warrants. "You're sure she can hear me?"

I smile at her radiant face. "Absolutely sure."

8

AS MUCH FUN AS
CHRISTMAS

It's a week before Christmas, and we've been giving our surplus money away as if we were St. Nicholas on a binge. Every morning there is a line of people waiting at the door when we arrive. After we open, the phone would have been ringing constantly if not for the advantage of our having only one line.

We are in the middle of preparing Christmas baskets for some of our struggling clients. The baskets are actually Christmas sixty-gallon trash bags filled with toys for the children and grocery vouchers for a holiday meal.

Earlier this week, after they got out of school for the winter break, my two daughters helped us select and wrap stuffed animals and games for the families on our list. It was so exciting for the girls to do this that they pronounced that it was "almost as much fun as Christmas." My fellow Vincentians, at first doubtful that children would be much help, eventually admitted it was useful to have eight- and ten-year-olds' opinions during the selection of toys for other eight- and ten-year-olds.

Today is the last day the store will be open before the holiday. It is noon, and we still have ten sacks of gifts waiting to be picked up by the selected families. I have called all the people on our list, but this demographic of the needy tends to have a disproportionate number of phones that either have been disconnected or are simply a neighbor's line where we must leave a message. These situations require some caution.

"Tammy doesn't live there? Oh, I see. Well, could you tell her that St. Vincent de Paul called and that she needs to pick up a package at the store by three o'clock? She'll know what it is and . . . tell her she needs to bring photo I.D. with her, okay?"

First thing in the morning, Gene, our president, comes out of the office and says to me, "We've only got three hundred and thirty-five bucks in the checkbook, and it's not nearly what we usually give away. Say a prayer that it will cover what we need to help the people who come in today. I don't know what else to do."

I'm in the Christmas mood, and this news has a dampening effect. But then I remember that the first Christmas wasn't all jolliness and ho, ho, ho for the people involved in it, either. I think to myself, *Did Joseph ask Mary to say a prayer for enough money to pay the new tax when they set off for Bethlehem?*

I have completed all the reminder phone calls. Now it is a matter of waiting and hoping that our clients will be able to "come and get it." Meanwhile, I walk out of the back room onto the sales floor to check if Dorothy needs me at the cash register. She points out a middle-aged woman. "Why don't you see if that lady needs some help? She's been wandering around the store for quite some time but hasn't found anything to buy yet."

The woman is about my own age, older by five years or so. Or maybe it is just the heaviness of her worn, over-stuffed winter coat that makes her look so dragged down. At first, she shakes her head when I ask her if there is anything I can help her with, but then she says, "They told me sometimes you people help out new mothers who need baby things." She pauses, noting something in my facial expression. "It's not for me, it's for my daughter—she's seventeen." A sigh and a shrug. "She just had the baby yesterday, and she doesn't have anything for it."

She doesn't smile at the mention of a new grandchild. It is a complicated blessing that has come upon this woman who is too young to be a grandmother and too old for the type of mothering she is being called upon to do.

"Sometimes we do that," I say carefully, remembering the overstretched checkbook, not wanting to raise her hopes too high.

Our resources extend from providing clothing, household items, and blankets to financial help with back rent and utility bills, but it is never enough. No matter how much we distribute to needy people, their crises are never fully subdued. The moment always comes when we have to say, "You may have these or those things, but not that." The great strain of helping the poor is that, at some point, we always are forced to say "no more." We can never give all they obviously lack.

"What kinds of things does she need?" I ask this sad grandmother.

"She's got no crib . . . and clothes and a blanket, diapers, bottles—just about everything." There are tears shining from her eyes.

All of a sudden it is a week before the first Christmas. *Is this what St. Anne felt like when she was helping pack Mary's bags for the trip to Bethlehem?*

"Okay," I say too quickly, in order to cut off her litany of hopes. Hopes, I'm afraid, can't be filled. "Take a seat with those other people waiting at the back of the store. You can talk to our president. He'll tell you what we can do for your daughter."

I lift a belated prayer for the checkbook and go back to help at the cash register.

About an hour and several clients later, Gene comes out of the office with the woman and tells me to help her find baby things. The lady seems calmer but still unutterably tired. Together we gather sleepers, socks, undershirts, a hat, blankets, crib sheets, and even a snowsuit. It is a lot, but there is no crib to give her. We always have to say "no" somewhere.

Is this how Joseph felt when he put clean straw in the manger?

The corners of the new grandmother's mouth lift just a little as I write down the items for our records and fold them into bags. As I hand it all over to her, she says, "I'll be back on Saturday for the washer and dryer. The man in the office said I could have the ones in the back room. I think I can get my neighbor to haul them for me in his truck. You'll hold them for me until then?"

"Not a problem. I'll put your name on them."

Gene is smiling that afternoon when he is at last finished with all the clients who have come for help.

"Take a guess how much the checks I wrote added up to," he says.

"How much?"

"Three hundred and forty exactly. I threw in the extra five from my wallet."

We both laugh.

"You gave away almost that much in that washer and dryer," I note.

He squirms. "We could have sold those appliances in a minute. The money would have paid a few bills but sometimes..." He shrugs. "When it comes to babies, I'm helpless."

Was that what the innkeeper said?

Finally, it is three o'clock, time to close the store. All the volunteers are ready to go home and start preparing for the great feast of Jesus' birth. But we have one Christmas trash bag left.

I try again to call the family who has requested the gifts, but no one answers the phone. The black sack holds wrapped packages for a two-year-old boy and a food gift certificate for his mom and grandma.

We have tried phoning them for three days. We shrug our shoulders and put on our coats. Sometimes it seems like we go to an awful lot of bother for people who don't appreciate it. Too bad, but what more can we do?

The phone rings. Jesus' timing was inconvenient two thousand years ago and he hasn't improved much on that since. Gene, Dorothy and I look at each other. Not everybody wants to be a hero. Someone (I won't mention names) picks up the receiver.

Of course it is the mom for the leftover basket.

We all sigh.

Her little boy is in the hospital. He had emergency surgery three days ago. His prognosis looks good, but he won't be released until Christmas Day. Is it too late to get the basket?

"Which hospital?"

"What's the room number?"

My coworkers pack up the leftover holiday cookies we had brought to share with each other and tuck them in with the gifts.

When we walk into the hospital room, we are greeted like welcome friends. Mom and Grandma are doing their best, but a two-year-old with an I.V. line strapped to his arm is not an easy person to deal with. Young Isaiah is bouncing around the room, alternately tugging at the contraption on his arm and tangling the tubing in hopeless loops. He opens the gifts instantly; never were distractions more needed.

Mom and Grandma are ravenous and half the goodies disappear while we watch. They thank us over and over again. The gift certificate for food is tucked gratefully away for later.

As we walk down the hospital corridor, I can't help agreeing with my young daughters that this truly brings as much joy as Christmas itself.

Is that what the three Wise Men said to each other as they climbed back on their camels leaving their gifts behind?

9

WHAT'S A WELCOME WORTH?

My good friend Bess and I are discussing charitable giving over cups of tea at her kitchen table. Her small congregation of Mennonites has decided to donate thirty brand new box fans to the St. Vincent de Paul Society.

"Box fans?" I am puzzled.

"Yes," she nods. "We wanted to do something this summer to prevent child abuse."

I sip my tea and ponder for a while. Eventually I say, "I'm not really following your thinking on this."

She waves her hand through the muggy Michigan air. "Hot nights, crying babies, sleepless parents—and we didn't have a lot of money so—box fans.

"Ah."

This is not just a sign of Mennonite practicality; it also shows their faith in St. Vincent de Paul's ability to reach the people who need help the most. Bess and her husband, Will, have contributed in countless ways to the Society's work since I have been volunteering there. Why not box fans?

Bess has been good for my spiritual growing pains. She listens sympathetically when I describe the frustration of my attempts to better organize the St. Vincent de Paul group. She nods, laughs, pats my hand and gives generously to the cause. Due to support from friends like her, and from my family, I have continued volunteering despite many frustrations.

Another reason I keep going is that we have been strangely successful in recruiting new volunteers. The store is now open five days a week all year round with a different crew working each day. In addition, we visit the local Catholic high school a couple of times a year to tell our stories of battling poverty. The teenagers have become a regular source of muscles and enthusiasm. This influx of new blood has been inspiring for all of us.

Yet, invariably, new volunteers take one look around and offer to help get us organized. They have no idea how much I have labored to get the place looking and running like an efficient organization that deserves the title "organization." Most of our newcomers voice serious doubts about trying to run a charity with nothing but constantly rotating volunteers, one phone line, fluctuating hours of operation, a leaky roof, and prayer.

I wonder about all that too.

It's not only that we've been known to sell the same couch to three different people, or that we forget to pay the sales tax to the government, or schedule too many clients for the same interview slots. All of that happens pretty regularly. The main reason I have my doubts about our competence to be running a charity is that we are so obviously flawed.

Some of us, for instance, don't like dealing with poor people.

Some of us don't like to be addressed in any language but English.

Some of us want nothing to do with alcoholics and drug addicts.

Most of us are wary of recently released prisoners.

Some of us are prejudiced.

Some of us become openly irritable with donors who give us junk.

We have been known to argue with each other in front of the clients and to argue with the clients as well.

The cash register doesn't always balance, and neither does the checkbook.

The store shelves are in a state of perpetual flux between too much stuff crammed onto them and "throw everything into the dumpster!"

The volunteers who know how to change the light fuses, and the ones who know how to change the cash-register tape, are never the people on duty when the store goes dark and the paper receipts turn pink.

Most days it seems as if we are going about helping the poor in the most inefficient way possible, and yet it works. Every week we are paying utility shut-off notices, preventing evictions, chipping in for prescription meds, helping pay for funerals, clothing people, delivering furniture and appliances, and attempting to reintegrate former prisoners into the community.

Pondering all this over our cups of tea, I ask my friend Bess, "What does it mean to be charitable? Sometimes, in the middle of the stress of running the store and helping people with overdue bills, it feels like we are just bumbling along without a clear goal."

Bess is an organized thinker. It doesn't take long before she gives me three categories into which she splits this intrinsic Christian virtue.

"Well, first," she says, "there is the 'recycling' type of charitable work. This is when I give away something I don't want or need. For instance, when I give my old clothes to St. Vincent de Paul, it is because I don't want them anymore. I feel better giving them away than throwing them out, and there is the chance that someone else can use them."

I think about that definition and decide that a lot of what we do at St. Vinnie's is actually recycling.

"The second type of giving is what we could characterize as 'sharing,'" she continues. "For instance, we have extra money so we give thirty box fans to help people who can't buy one for themselves. When we donate money to the church, or any other charity for that matter, we've shared our resources, but we haven't impoverished ourselves to the point of suffering."

Okay . . . Sharing accounts for the rest of what we do at St. Vincent de Paul.

"And the third type of charity is like this; all I have is one box fan for myself on a very hot day, but—here, take it—it's yours."

"But," I protest, "that's like Jesus' poor woman who gave her last two pennies, or like what he said about 'the greatest love is to give up one's life for another.' We don't even come close to that at St. Vinnie's."

"Yes," she agrees, "I think true charity is very rare. And it can appear in the least likely people."

I realize that she is absolutely right about this.

I tell Bess about the bed dealer.

He is the fellow who comes into our resale shop about once a month to look over the used furniture and offer us low bids on the beds.

In the normal course of events, we either sell the beds and then give the money away, or we give the beds away—both results fit our goal as a charity to help people in need.

But this bed dealer doesn't fit the categories of who we want to help. Need is the key word here. Because this fellow is a used furniture dealer, he has a little resale business of his own. Anything he buys from us is sure to be sold across town for a profit. Somehow it rubs the wrong way that he is making money off the things we sell to him. But we can't very well put signs on the beds that say, "For Sale to Non-Dealers Only." That would be a non-welcoming sort of attitude. Besides, antique dealers, collectors, and eBay types shop at our store every day, and we take their money without a grumble. It's just that beds are so scarce.

I confess to Bess that most of the time we are not very welcoming when the bed dealer walks into our store. On one particular day, we start to rethink our bad attitude.

One of our mentally ill customers comes into the shop and asks us for some free clothing. He lives in a community-funded group apartment, supervised by live-in social workers. It is only a couple of blocks from the store, so we see him and his housemates frequently. Today the volunteers give him several jogging suits along with some towels, and then they write down the items for our records. In the process they notice that we have just given him the identical items the day before. It's right in our records, clear as day. They bring him to me.

Usually we wouldn't give someone clothing two days in a row because that would be a clear signal to our clients that laundromats are for losers.

"We just gave you jogging suits and towels yesterday," I tell him.

"Yes, I like them. I want some more, please."

"But we can't give you clothes every day."

"Oh, I see. Can I have more clothes tomorrow?"

This gentleman is so badly afflicted by his illness that he is not capable of comprehending my logical, or even rational, explanations. I tell him to sit down and wait while I go and get our Society president, Gene.

Gene interviews him in the privacy of the office for twenty minutes and then he comes out, takes me aside and says, "Here's the list of things we gave him yesterday. Give him whatever he wants within reason."

I look at the paper he hands me and ask, "Does that mean, don't give him what's on this list?"

He looks at me in frustration. "Oh, for crying out loud—he wants the exact same things, so I guess you may as well let him have them. It doesn't make any sense, but that's what he wants."

So I catch up with our client among the jogging suits and help him find the clothing he wants, which isn't easy. He keeps choosing items that are four or five sizes too small. In the end, he goes away with three jogging suits (one of which doesn't fit but he likes the color), some hand towels, and a pair of patent-leather dancing shoes. He refuses to try these on because he is sure that they will be "just right."

We are closed the following day but Gene and I are working Saturday when he reappears in the shop. We both see him coming and retreat into the back room, out of sight.

We can hear his loud, flat-sounding voice. He keeps repeating, "Can I have some clothes? Can I have some clothes?" to everyone in the shop, unable to make any distinction between customers and workers. After a brief spell of cowardice, Gene sighs and returns to the sales floor to help him once again.

He comes back laughing. "Guess what happened?" he asks me.

"He wants more jogging suits and towels?"

"I don't know what he wants. But what happened was that our old friend, the bed dealer, reached into his wallet and gave him a twenty to buy some clothes and he took it and left."

"He did?"

"Yeah, and the dealer wasn't even upset that he didn't buy any clothes with it. He just shrugged and smiled."

"Wow. Who'd have thought that the bed guy—of all people . . .?"

"It doesn't surprise me. He's really not a bad person."

So, under Bess's definition, St. Vincent de Paul—officially a charity in anyone's book—we are "recycling." And the used-furniture dealer—despised profiteer—he was "sharing." And the client? He gave us all he had—his story.

Why am I so critical of the bed dealer, anyway? He does what any ordinary person does in a thrift store—he hunts for bargains. And from all appearances, it looks as if we are running a thrift store at St. Vincent de Paul.

At our meetings we frequently get into discussions about how better to run the store. Should we raise our prices? Give away less? Not accept so many donations? Lock our dumpster? Move to a better retail location? All these issues would come up with any resale shop.

Eventually, it occurs to us that our purpose is not to run the most profitable, shrewd, efficient, riff-raff-free store in town. Our purpose is to help the poor and to change our own way of thinking and being. It only looks as though we run a store.

The store is just our cover.

It's such an ingenious disguise that we fool a lot of people, sometimes even ourselves.

One Saturday in January, a young woman comes rushing in. She is crying. She tells Jim and Bonnie that her friend's baby is very sick and needs to see a doctor. She has no car, no money for a cab or an ambulance, and it is eight degrees outside. Our volunteers have to make a quick decision. They would have to close the store in order to take this mother and baby to the medical clinic. What to do? They drive her to the clinic, of course.

After all, we're not running a store. The young woman has seen through our cover, and it only takes our volunteers a moment to realize it.

After they deliver mother and baby to the hospital, Jim and Bonnie drive back to the shop and unlock the door. They walk back behind the cash register and pretend to be store clerks again.

Just like after church every Sunday, millions of Christians walk back out into their neighborhoods and pretend to be ordinary citizens again. We're not. It's just our cover.

My husband, Dean, is catching on to this idea faster than I am. He has always been a caring, generous person, but as his involvement with St. Vincent de Paul deepens, the ordinary-citizen disguise becomes easier and easier for people to see through.

One morning on his way to work, he is pumping gas into his car, unhappy about the rising prices and feeling helpless to control the blur of dollars that flash by on the meter.

A woman's voice calls out behind him as he screws in the gas cap. "Hey, mister."

He cranes his head around. She is standing about thirty feet away on the sidewalk near the street. He scans the parking lot wondering who she means, but there doesn't seem to be any other "misters" nearby.

"Pardon?" he asks.

"Hey, mister. You going downtown?"

It happens that he is headed that way, but he hesitates, wondering where this is leading. She begins a long explanation of the crisis she is in the midst of, walking toward him as she speaks.

Obviously, Dean is no longer incognito.

Being a volunteer for the St. Vincent de Paul Society, he has heard many, many such convoluted stories involving sleepless nights on the street, ex-friends who leave people stranded, too much walking, and maybe too much alcohol. After listening for a short time, he says to her, "Do you need a ride?"

No more is necessary. She jumps into the back seat. He climbs into the front and turns on the engine, and studies his unexpected passenger in the mirror as she does the same to him. She is middle-aged, has a lovely name that means "light" and the ability to fill up a conversation with no prompting. After hearing more than he wants to know about her personal previous twenty-four hour history, he pulls out into traffic and asks her, "Where do you want me to take you?"

"Park and Westnedge," she says, but her voice catches on the street names. He looks at her in the rearview mirror and sees that she is crying.

He hands her his handkerchief over his shoulder. "Those two streets are parallel to each other," he tells her gently.

"Oh. Are they?" She wipes her entire face with the soft cloth. "The bus station, then. What street is that on? Can you take me there?"

"Sure," he says.

She begins sobbing into the hanky.

He takes the pear beside him on the seat, which he had snatched from the kitchen counter in his rush out the door, and hands it to her. "Would you like some breakfast?"

She thanks him and devours half the fruit in seconds and tucks the other half into her pocket, but this doesn't slow down the constant stream of explanations. "I work so long and so hard and someone always pulls me back down. People are all out for themselves and they don't care what happens to nobody else. And church people are the worst. It's like they don't want to be dirtied up with people's problems. I'll never go back to churches to ask for help again, they treat me so bad. But someone like you, who has no reason to help, you just put me in your car and ask, 'where you want to go?'—that's why I'm crying."

"But I belong to a church," he says. "Have you ever heard of the St. Vincent de Paul Society?"

She nods her head slowly. "Yeah, yeah, that little store, you mean? They helped me a while back when my rent was overdue."

"I volunteer there a couple of times a month. Those are church people."

"Well, now, I guess you're right about that. They had a lot of religious stuff in the place anyway."

For obvious reasons he thinks it would be a good thing to change her tactics about where to find a ride, so he cautiously continues with his street-corner apologetics.

"I lost my job four years ago," he tells her. "Being a part of a church meant that there were people around me to pick me up when I was down. All I'm saying is: don't give up on the people who might be your best support."

She nods and wipes her eyes again as he pulls the car into the bus station and that is the end of the story.

Or maybe not.

I am beginning to understand that charity is not something I do in my spare time under controlled conditions. And it is not even something that I do particularly well. For instance, I learn a huge lesson in charitable giving from a bank teller.

Whenever I cash my paycheck, the teller at my branch performs the requested transactions, then pauses, and always asks me, "Is there anything else I can do for you today?"

Usually I answer in the negative, but once in a while I remember something I've forgotten—a new check register, the balance in my accounts, etc. What's most important is that it's nice to be asked.

Well-trained waitstaff at restaurants ask this question in a different way. "Ketchup? More napkins? Warm your coffee?" Paying customers expect this simple courtesy.

But, in God's eyes, aren't we all non-paying customers?

One day at St. Vincent de Paul, a client needs money for a prescription drug. It is for pain medication. She has a problem because she has recently been released from prison and her parole officer warned her that any narcotic detected in her system would be a violation of her parole. So a doctor has prescribed a non-narcotic, but she can't afford it.

This is a bit tricky. Being a low-budget operation, we don't have a fax. Before I can comply with her request, I ask her to bring a copy of the prescription from the pharmacy, which is located four blocks away. While she is gone, I phone the social worker at her doctor's office and also the pharmacist to verify everything she has told me.

Her story checks out, so I write a check to the pharmacy to give to our client when she returns. Keep in mind that she has no car, is experiencing considerable pain, and it is twenty degrees outside.

By the time she comes back with the prescription, I am feeling like a brute. I thank her for the effort she has made for the sake of our procedures. Then I pause, and say, "Is there anything else I can do for you today?"

She looks stunned.

Her expression collapses into tearful gratitude. The answer is yes; she needs eyeglasses. I give her the number of the Lion's Club. She has never heard of them.

"Anything else?"

Her utility bill is overdue. I make an appointment for her to come back the following week with the shut-off notice.

She is blown away by simple customer courtesy. She shakes my hand, thanking me over and over again. I guess she doesn't go to my bank.

So I begin to see that maybe even our humble "recycling" and "sharing" types of charity can benefit from a little fine-tuning. There is something crucial about the simple type of courtesy that Dorothy showed to the drunken man that first day I stepped into the shop.

I get a mighty lesson one day while I am interviewing a client in the office.

The young woman walks into the St. Vincent de Paul office and loses control of her overstuffed folder. Identification documents, receipts, bills, court edicts, and who knows what else spill in every direction.

While another volunteer stoops to pick up the tangle of paper, I put out my hand. "Hi, I'm Jane. What can we help you with today?"

She sifts through the pile, "I need help with the first-month's deposit on an apartment. I've already been to some other churches, but I can't remember the exact amount that the worker at the other place promised me. It's here somewhere."

If I'm going to help her, I will need exact numbers. I watch her go through the papers two more times before I say, "Why don't I call and have them look up your file?"

She sighs gratefully and tells me her story as I dial the phone.

She has recently extracted herself from an abusive marriage, has found a home for herself and her two young daughters, is working and taking college classes. She is only twenty-three years old. Small wonder she has lost some paperwork.

I ask to speak to the worker at a very busy church office. After being connected, when I request the information about our client, I get an earful instead.

"She can't find the papers I gave her?" the worker snaps at me. "I've copied them twice already! She is such a flake, and I don't care if she hears me say it. I don't know how that girl expects me to keep copying things for her all the time!"

I thank her for the number and hang up quickly. The young woman in front of me has a face of stone.

She has heard.

We pretend she hasn't.

As I fill out yet another form for her to keep track of, I ask her if she belongs to a church. She doesn't. She hasn't found one that feels welcoming.

I think about that for a moment. "You know how it says in the Bible 'Ask and you will receive' but it doesn't mean we'll get everything we ask for?"

She shakes her head, "Not in my life."

"What it does mean, I think, is that you have to ask. We want signs from God. But God wants a sign too. He needs to know that you believe he exists."

A tear rolls down her cheek. I pat her knee and give her a tissue. "Try this," I say. "Go into a church, any church, even an empty one, and tell God all the problems you told me."

What am I thinking, giving her this advice? After all, the poor woman has just been verbally abused in front of me by someone from a church-based organization. I guess my purpose is that I desperately don't want to be a part of the shunning she has experienced. I want her to know that she is welcome in God's house whenever she is ready.

I am grateful when she accepts a prayer card along with our promissory note for money. I'm glad when she allows me to tape some crucial information to the front of her overstuffed folder. I tell her I admire how she is shouldering so many responsibilities.

She doesn't reject me the same way she has been rejected.

Instead, a tear slips down her cheek.

I don't know if she will ever go into a church, but if she does, I hope that someone will be there to welcome her.

I hope they welcome her even if she doesn't fit the image of the type of person they want to help.

I hope that if she needs a ride, she doesn't stop some stranger in a gas station but knocks on a church door instead.

And I hope someone is there to say, "What else can we do for you today?"

10

WHOSE POPE IS HE,
ANYWAY?

Spring approaches and thoughts of Lent, Easter, and First Communion fill my head. Even though I'm a cradle Catholic, for the first time in my life I am now more fully aware of the seasons on the Church calendar than the seasons outside the church window. After pouring over catalogs all winter and listening to countless religious gift salesmen, I have taught myself how to stock the shelves with merchandise that a few short months ago I couldn't even properly identify.

For instance, now I know the difference between the green scapular and the brown scapular. I can look at a rosary and tell a customer whether it is aurora borealis crystal or cut glass. Someone suffers from depression? St. Dymphna is the gal I recommend. Need a statue of Mary? Our Lady of Grace is a perennial favorite. I can tell the difference between a pyx and a rosary box, and can distinguish rhodium plate from pewter on the St. Christopher medals. Customers discuss with me their theological preferences for crucifixes over crosses and vice versa.

When it comes to idiosyncrasies and peculiarities, I am more Catholic than I have ever been in my life. And people are beginning to notice.

I'm not sure if that is a good thing.

I am helping a very nice lady who needs some night-gowns because she will be admitted to the hospital for major surgery the next day, and she wants some nice things to wear other than the half-gowns they give out.

While I am writing up the donation record, she leans close to me and quietly asks, "May I ask you something personal?"

I assure her that I am fine with that.

"Are you a Catholic?" she says shyly.

"Yes. Yes, I am."

She leans even closer and inquires seriously, "Do you believe in Jesus?"

My eyebrows go up for a fraction of a second, and then I calm myself and confide, "Yes, I do. In fact, he's the reason we're here helping people."

"I thought so!" she says with a note of satisfaction. "I don't believe everything I hear, you know. Some people, they say that the Catholics don't believe in Jesus—that they only believe in Mary—but I saw all those crosses hanging behind you on the wall there and I said to myself, 'Uh-uh, they must be telling me a line.' It's just no good believing everything that you hear, is it?"

I am without words to respond to such an astonishing rumor.

One of our other customers, who is in the process of purchasing some Catholic children's books and has overheard our conversation, tells her emphatically, "I'm very glad you don't believe everything you hear!"

I finish bagging the nightgowns and hand the package to our client. She smiles at me uncertainly, "I didn't offend you, did I, honey? I just thought I should find out for myself about all the stories people tell."

"Not at all," I answer. "Please ask anything you like—it clears up a lot of confusion."

She agrees wholeheartedly with me, and I wish her the best of outcomes on her surgery.

After she leaves, I ponder: What is a Catholic if not a believer in Jesus?

How come our neighbors don't know that we are Christians?

This looks bad.

My next encounter of this kind delivers another bewildering moment.

I am dusting the Bibles that we carry in the shop. A middle-aged lady, who has just finished purchasing some used clothing, notices what I am doing and asks if she might see one of the Bibles.

"Yes, of course. Which one would you like to see?"

Her eyes widen. "You have more than one kind of Bible?"

"Sure," I answer easily, unaware of the controversy I have just muddled into. "There's the New American, which is the translation you'll hear at Mass. Then there is the Jerusalem Bible, which uses more poetic language with an extensive system of footnotes. And we also have the Revised Standard Version in a Catholic edition." I take pride in spewing out my new knowledge.

"No King James Bibles at all?"

"King James? Um . . . no, sorry."

She shakes her head slowly. "I heard that you all don't have the real Bible. But where did you get these other ones?"

It is obvious that she thinks she is in the presence of the worst kind of heretic, but I try to explain anyway. "See . . . actually . . . we never had the King James Bible because it's a translation that appeared after the Reformation."

"After the what?"

Her question is painful for me, but for my husband, who is a Lutheran, it might have been excruciating. I am glad he is not here.

I explain that the Reformation was the time in the sixteenth century when the Protestant churches broke away from the Catholic church, and it was after that split that the King James Version came into use. "So we never had that translation," I finish.

She is clearly astounded by all this history, but doesn't lose focus on the central issue.

"What Bible did you have before all this breakup happened?"

"The Vulgate. It was a Latin translation from the fifth century."

"And you use that?"

"No, we use an English translation now."

"May I see one?"

"Of course." I hand her the New American Bible, which she opens and begins to read.

After only a few lines, she looks at me with a surprised expression. "This is just like reading a story! It's almost like people talk."

"It's more modern language than the King James," I admit.

"It might be nice to have one of these to just read at home. Is it the whole Bible?"

"Oh, yes, plus a few more books that you might not be used to."

"*More* books?" She closes it disapprovingly and hands it back to me almost sadly. "I guess it's true then, that you all don't have the real Bible."

I try to explain about the other books, but the whole Reformation idea is a suspicious story to her already. I fail to convince her that we haven't been in the business of making up our own bit of fiction and calling it God's Word. As she leaves the store, she is shaking her head.

Sigh.

The next time I encounter a person who has never met a Catholic, I will send them to the experts, the Catholics who are at the top of their game. Why are people asking me these questions, anyway? I'm just a thrift store volunteer.

A college-age couple comes into the store and requests help in finding a St. Benedict medal for the young man. Not having one in stock, I arrange to special-order the medal for them and in taking down the relevant information, we fall into conversation.

"We're so excited about finding your store." The young lady smiles shyly at me. "We had no idea that we could buy these things right here in town."

"Where are you from?"

"We're students at the university—in the graduate program in medieval studies. We graduate in April, and then we're going to get married." She blushes charmingly and smiles at her fiancé.

He squeezes her hand and turns to me. "We thought maybe we would get married in the church that's across the parking lot, but we couldn't find anyone to talk to over there. But after looking around, we spotted your shop. Could you tell us how we inquire about getting married there?"

"The parish priest is where you would start, but if you want to get married this spring there might be a problem because of the required six-month engagement period."

"Six months! Is the building booked that much in advance?"

I explain about the diocesan requirements for marriage preparation.

"Oh," she says in comprehension, "but we're not Catholic, so that wouldn't apply to us."

"At least one of you has to be Catholic to get married in a Catholic church," I inform them gently. I give them a quick overview of the idea of the sacraments and how the church defines itself and its members that way. This is genuinely new information for them, but they seem to be accepting of the idea.

"We don't know anyone who is a Catholic, so could you tell us how to go about becoming one?"

Now it is my turn to be astonished. "If you don't know anyone who is Catholic, how much do you know about the Catholic church?"

"Quite a lot, actually," he assures me. "You see we were pagans—there is a large group of them at the university and they have regular gatherings every month and well, that's where we met." I study them with fresh curiosity, having never met any actual pagans before. I guess I have always assumed that the only ones that St. Patrick hadn't converted lived in places like Papua New Guinea or Hollywood.

The young man continues their story of conversion. "When we were discussing pagan rituals one time, one of the other members of our group told us that most of the ancient feasts had been stolen by the Catholic church and changed to fit Christianity. He was rather angry about it and in order to back up his arguments he mentioned some books in the Medieval Institute Library that describe some of the original customs and how they had been 'Christianized' and obliterated. So we looked them up one day, and it was fascinating. It didn't take long to realize that the Catholics had known about the pagan festivals for a long time and in actuality have incorporated them into their religion rather than wipe them out. So we just kept reading and eventually we came upon St. Benedict's Rule and, well—who wouldn't be Catholic after reading that?" He is speaking with frankness and respect, and she is nodding solemnly in agreement.

Since I know more about St. Benedict's medals than I know about his Rule, I nod vaguely and refrain from comment. But if the Rule of Benedict has been instrumental in converting this couple, I'm thinking that it is high time I get a copy. I wonder what other hidden diamonds I have missed?

"So," he continues, "How do we go about becoming Catholic?"

"Well, there is a series of classes that start in the fall and go through until Easter Sunday. But if you want to get married this spring, I guess you had better go talk to a priest." I give them the name of an open-hearted priest at a local parish and wish them luck, and they happily shake my hand in gratitude.

"None of our friends knew where we could get a St. Benedict medal," she says to me. "And now—finding this store and meeting a real Catholic—how cool is that?"

A real Catholic.

Is that who she sees in me?

It's certainly not the first definition I would give to myself. When I look at myself, I see a mother, a wife, a teacher, a daughter, a sister, a friend, a volunteer . . . What is a *real* Catholic, anyway?

I suspect most answers to that question are offensive to most Catholics.

Is a real Catholic the one who goes to church every Sunday? Or are the real Catholics the ones who perform acts of charity? Am I a real Catholic if I was baptized as a baby, or is it more authentic to come to the Church as the pagan couple did, full of awe, enthusiasm, and respect? We, like all Christians, believe in Jesus; that's certain. So is it our devotion to Mary that defines us as Catholics? Catholics respect and love the word of God in the Bible, but our Scriptures don't match our Christian brethren's. Do those few extra books in the Old Testament (which I can't even name with certainty) make me distinctively Catholic?

Perhaps it all comes down to the pope. If nothing else, we Catholics have a link to the man in Vatican City. We may not always see eye to eye with him, but that seems to bother the secular media more than it does us. Are we Catholics because the pope exists? Or does the pope exist because we are Catholics?

While I contemplate my denominational definition in the cosmos, one of our local homeless men comes into the shop. He has shoulder-length red hair and weathered skin. He is wearing tattered clothing, carries a worn backpack over his shoulder, and he speaks with the diction and vocabulary of a Harvard grad.

I greet him as I would any customer, but he only grumbles back at me suspiciously.

It's no secret that many of the people who live on the streets are coping with mental illness along with their homelessness. Though I don't like to assume anything, a sizeable percentage of our clients might possibly fall into this category. This particular gentleman strikes me in this way. I'm not trying to make a diagnosis—I think of it as an untrained laywoman's observation.

After looking around the store for a time, the gentleman becomes agitated and visibly upset by something in the display case where we keep the Bibles. When I ask if I can help him, he points to a small picture of John Paul II, and demands, "Who is that? Who do you think that is?"

"That's the pope," I say.

"The pope? The pope? *Whose* pope?"

"Umm . . . the Catholic's pope, I guess."

"Ha!" He shakes a finger at me. "He's not the Catholic's pope. He's everybody's pope. You don't own the pope. He's the world's pope. He belongs to all of us. And he's not a Catholic, either. Give me that picture. He's not yours."

I back off. Call it cowardice, but I can see no point in arguing. Even though I give him the picture, he rants a while longer. I just nod and try to calm him with assurances that John Paul II is certainly big enough to go around.

He takes the picture from my hand, tucks it carefully into his backpack, and leaves.

I have given away the pope without a fight.

Does that make me a *real* Catholic?

11

TIM

The young man is trying to decide between buying a pair of socks or a plastic change purse. The prices for such things in our store are in the category of two digits, but it seems that his funds are not up to a double purchase. He is wearing a bike helmet that is strapped tightly to his head. His clothing is clean and of good quality, and he looks well-cared for.

Not a street person, I conclude. Not visibly impoverished, either. So why the stress over mere pennies?

After debating with himself for several minutes, he asks Dorothy if she will hold the socks for a short time so that he can go to his bank and get the money he needs.

Dorothy offers to pay for the socks herself, but the young man refuses to let her. "You're an angel, Dorothy," he tells her. "You don't need to do that, but you sure are an angel. God hides his angels all over the place, and you're one of them."

"Oh, shush, Tim," she says and looks embarrassed. "I'm far from an angel."

But I see that Tim is spot-on about Dorothy, and I warm to him. "The socks are only a quarter," I point out.

"Take them with you and pay us back the next time you come in."

"Oh, no, no, no. I couldn't do that. If you just hold them for me, I'll be right back, I promise. It won't take me long. I only need to go to the bank, and I have plenty of money in my account." Before leaving, he pays Dorothy the dime for the change purse and then rushes outside to his waiting bike. He unlocks it in a hurry and pedals away.

In less than twenty minutes he returns, panting and perspiring from his ride, and he plunks a shiny new quarter on the counter.

Dorothy rings up the sale on the cash register and puts the socks in a bag. "It comes to twenty-seven cents with the tax," she tells him.

His face falls. He has forgotten about the sales tax.

I picture him peddling his bike to the bank, filling out the withdrawal slip, standing in line, and showing his I.D. I try to imagine the look on the teller's face. *All that for one quarter.*

He is upset with himself more than with us. "How could I make a mistake like that? After you've been so patient. I'm sorry about this. You held them for me and everything. I get so dumb sometimes."

Dorothy again offers to cover the difference herself, but that isn't going over any better than it did the first time.

"Oops," I say. "We forgot. No sales tax on socks. They're exempt."

Dorothy gives me a surprised look, but then she recovers. "Oh. Yes. That's right. No tax."

Tim's head pops up. "You're kidding me! Are you kidding me?"

"Nope. Our mistake. No sales tax on used socks."

"You're kidding me!"

"I could be wrong. I just started working here a few months ago so I get some of the rules mixed up sometimes, but I think that's right. No sales tax on used socks in the state of Michigan."

"What's your name? You're an angel, did you know that?"

I put out my hand. "I'm Jane. What's your name?"

"It's Tim. And I'm glad to know you, Jane. You're an angel. I'm always glad to meet an angel."

Blessed are you who are poor, for the kingdom of God is yours.

The next time Tim comes into the store, he is upset. It shows in his face, in his posture, in the sadness in his voice, everything about him.

"What's up, Tim? Something happen?"

"What's your name again? I remember you—you're an angel—but I can't remember your name."

"I'm Jane."

"Jane, of course. Hi Jane, I'm Tim. Someone stole my lock."

"Your lock? What was it locking?"

"My bike. They stole my bike lock. I can't believe it. What am I going to do without my lock? I can't leave my bike anywhere. Is it okay if I park it in front of the window like that? I'm so worried about leaving it in the parking lot."

I am confused. "They stole the lock, but they didn't steal the bike? How would that happen?"

"That's what I don't understand. Why would they steal my lock? It's no good to them because it's a combination lock, and they don't know the numbers. Why would they steal it?"

"Don't know, Tim. People do strange things. But, yeah, it's fine to leave your bike against the window."

Blessed are they who hunger and thirst for righteousness, for they will be satisfied.

One day Tim brings his mother into the shop to meet us. She is an elegant, white-haired lady trending toward late old age. Tim shows her around the store, excitedly pointing out the myriad of questionable treasures on the packed shelves. When she finds a spool of thread that she needs, he brings her selection to the counter and proudly purchases it for her.

"I've forgotten your name," he says. "I'm Tim. Is Dorothy here?"

"I'm Jane. No, Dorothy is off today, but I'll tell her you asked for her."

"Jane, this is my mom. She came shopping with me today. Mom, this is Jane. She's an angel."

Fearing to crush bones, I shake her hand as gently as I can. In her eyes, it is strikingly obvious where Tim's kindness originates.

"Tim is one of our favorite customers," I tell her. She looks pleased and proud.

Tim beams too. "She likes your store, Jane. Isn't that fantastic? I like it here, and my mom likes it here too. If Mom likes it, it must be a great place."

Wherever he has been cut short in life, Tim has come up trumps in the mother department, and he knows it.

Blessed are the pure of heart, for they will see God.

Life is changing for Tim. For a long stretch, we don't see him at all, and then he starts coming into the store with a hired caregiver in tow, a different one every week. Dorothy and I look these people over pretty carefully at first. Sometimes they are college-age kids. Most of them seem genuinely to care about him. We decide that they're okay.

There are no more runs to the bank when he needs small change, and he no longer wears the crash helmet or rides his bike. He doesn't get mugged now.

I can't help but smile when he walks in with his latest guardian. "Hi'ya, Tim. How's it going?"

"Great. It's going great. What's your name? Is it Linda?"

"It's Jane."

"Of course, I knew that. Jane, this is Linda, she drives me around to places I need to go."

Linda and I shake hands.

"Jane is an angel," he assures her. Then he turns to me. "Jane, you must have the most wonderful husband in the whole world. I bet you do, don't you?"

"Well, yes . . . Yes, as a matter of fact, my husband is pretty wonderful. How did you know that?"

"Because whenever I see you, you are always smiling. You are such a happy person that it must be that you have a husband who really loves you. You are so lucky."

When Tim leaves, I call Dean at work to tell him how wonderful he is. I haven't done this in a long time. My wonderful husband is amused and pleased at the same time.

Blessed are the peacemakers, for they will be called children of God.

Dorothy and I have been praying several weeks for Tim's stepfather, who is very ill. Tim asked us to do this and we are glad to, even though we have never met the gentleman.

When his stepfather dies, Tim comes into the store to tell us, and we offer our sympathy and more prayers. He is grateful. He is also very sad.

"How is your mom?" I ask him.

"She's a strong woman, Jane. This is very hard on her, but she is strong and I know she'll be all right."

"Were you close to your stepfather, Tim?"

He wipes at his eyes. "He was a good man, Jane. A good man . . ."

I give Tim a hug. He's a good man too.

Blessed are they who mourn, for they will be comforted.

12

ORDINARY DAYS

It is Ordinary Time on the church calendar, which means the banners in church are green and the priest's vestments are also green. It is that long stretch of time between the seasons of Easter and Advent, when the vividness of faith can muddle into the background of my life. Green is an appropriate fused color for this time of year, somewhere between the primary hues of blue and yellow. It is the unremarkable color of the small patch of grass in front of the store, the color of the summer leaves on the maple tree next to the curb, and the color of the checks in the St. Vincent de Paul checkbook.

This is an ordinary day in Ordinary Time, and I am an ordinary Christian who is writing some checks to help people who are in financial distress. There is no royal purple kingdom-building going on here, and there is no martyr-red splashed across my desk, either. The things I do at the St. Vincent de Paul shop are not draped in vivid colors.

But the things that happen on any given ordinary day almost always are.

First thing in the morning, I write a check for a woman who needs a copy of her wedding license in order to prove who she is so she can donate plasma and get enough money for food. She has just been released from jail, so she also asks for some free clothing. We allow her to pick out what she wants from the racks. She chooses high heels, two frilly dresses, and a negligee. We don't ask why she was in jail.

After she leaves, the neighborhood homeless shelter calls and wants to know if we will buy the bus ticket for a woman whose doctor wants her to go to the Cleveland Clinic immediately. The Department of Human Services will cover expenses like this for homeless people, but their process requires days—not immediately. The doctor doesn't want her to wait that long. We send the check over to the bus station.

The next man waiting to see us is blurry-eyed with toothache, and asks if we will help him come up with thirty-five dollars. The county health department will remove his tooth for that amount, which is a deal compared to a private dental clinic, so we agree to cover the expense for him.

No one else is in line for help, so I put away the checkbook and go into the sorting room to help Laura with the pricing. She is a new volunteer and might need some tips on how things operate. We haven't been at it long before we are interrupted.

A man strides mission-like through the front door, asks directions at the cash register, and heads toward us. This gentleman is looking good. The sport coat is tailored, the sweater like new, the shoes are polished, and the briefcase is leather. He walks into the back room and glances around. Laura and I look up from the merchandise that we are pricing. He seems out of place the way he is dressed, as if someone gave him the wrong address, so I ask, "Can we help you?"

"Do you accept clothing donations here?"

"Yes."

"Sweaters? Do you take men's sweaters?" He seems to be in a hurry.

"We sure do." Laura says. "Are they in your car? Do you need help bringing them in?"

"No." He sets down his briefcase on the floor and removes his sport coat, then lays it on our table. Crossing his arms at his waist, he stretches his sweater over his head, shakes it right side out, and folds it neatly.

"Is this okay? Will you take it as is? It's clean. I just put it on this morning because it was chilly, but I don't want this sweater. Can I leave it with you folks?"

Laura and I exchange disbelieving looks. "I . . . guess so . . . ?" she says.

"Would you like a receipt?" I ask.

"No, thank you," he says, putting on his coat again.

Laura is biting the inside of her cheeks. She is so new at St. Vinnie's that she still half-expects our days to be ordinary. I wink at her and work hard at keeping a straight face while the gentleman buttons his coat.

Even if a bit unconventional, he seems like a generous sort of person. I figure there's nothing like trying. "Um . . . Sir, what we really could use are some men's shoes . . ."

He looks down at his feet, then back up at us, and smiles. "No," he says. "I'm afraid you're just getting the sweater today. Maybe another time." He turns around and leaves without a backward glance.

"I just have one question," I say to Laura as we watch him go.

"Just one?" she asks.

At noon, I sit down at the break table with Dorothy to eat my lunch. If I can, I like to get her talking about her childhood. Today she tells me about her father's first car. On hot summer nights, for an adventure, her dad would crank-start the Ford and take the whole family for a drive to a nearby lake for an evening swim.

"He would roll back the isinglass windows on the car so we could feel the breeze. The wind coming through was wonderful—of course, this was before anybody had air-conditioning or even fans."

"What were isinglass windows?" I ask.

She frowns. "I'm not sure what they were . . . I think they were made out of fish bladders. Anyway, they were foggy panels of stiff, see-through material. Very drafty in the winter. I'm glad we have real glass windows now."

Cars with fish-bladder windows? I have never heard of it before.

"And after we were done swimming, for a treat," she says, her expression smiling and far away, "my father would stop at the dairy on the corner of Lovers Lane and Kilgore."

I grin back at her. "My dad used to take us to the Dairy Queen for ice-cream cones in the summer too."

She shakes her head. "Oh, no. Ice cream was a luxury in those days. This was a real dairy with cows and barns."

"At Lovers Lane and Kilgore?" I am picturing the present-day five-lane-wide intersection.

She flaps a hand mildly. "That was way out in the country in those days. We would stop at the dairy farm, and my father would buy us each a piece of cheese. I can still remember how good it tasted on a hot July night."

"A piece of cheese? For a treat? Really?"

"Nothing better," she says, nodding. "I had a wonderful father, and he wasn't a Catholic, you know. The nuns at school used to tell us that non-Catholics couldn't go to heaven. That would upset us kids a lot."

My eyebrows go up. "I can imagine it would."

She presses her lips together momentarily, but then she chuckles softly. "Mother told us, 'Don't you fret about your father going to heaven. Sister doesn't know everything that God knows.'"

I smile. "You had a good mother too."

"Yes," she says. "I have a lot to be grateful for."

After lunch, the ordinary trend continues.

We are visited by a large group of Mennonite or Amish women (I didn't ask which) on a shopping spree. They arrive in an oversized van pulling an enclosed trailer that they park illegally on the street in front of the store. When they walk in the door, they each pick up a shopping basket and spread out in every direction.

"Good afternoon, Ladies," I say. They nod and smile in return, commenting in their German dialect among themselves. Three of them go to the back wall and start piling shoes into their baskets. They select nearly every pair of black shoes that we have—men's, women's, and children's. Only the high heels and strappy sandals are left on the shelves. They also load up on jigsaw puzzles, piling the boxes high on the checkout counter. Surprisingly, even though they are all dressed in unpatterned, homemade, shin-length dresses, they purchase quite a lot of our clothing, too, mostly men's cotton shirts, snow pants, and jackets.

As they are checking out, one of them asks me in English, "Do you know where the Goodwill thrift store is located? We went to the old store, and it is all closed up."

I tell them where our competitors moved and start to give the directions to the new store, when one of them interrupts, "Oh, we just needed the address." She pulls out a handheld GPS device and types in the street number. The other ladies look over her shoulder, and they discuss the route they will take to the rest of the second-hand stores in town. They adjust their white bonnets, smile their thanks, and leave the store as a group.

Dorothy says to me, "What was that gadget they were using? I never saw anything like it before."

While I try to explain GPS systems to Dorothy, our fellow volunteer, Jim, leaves on his errand to collect the money from the poor box in the back of the church. He does this once a week.

Today, when he returns, his face is white, and his breathing seems a little hypoxic. "Lock the doors," he says.

"What's wrong?" I follow him into the office.

"You'll never believe what just happened!" He bars the office door. Turning to me and uncoiling his fingers, he holds out a tightly rolled wad of bills. I take them and smooth them flat on the desk.

Green Franklins. Ten of them.

"Where'd you find these?" I ask.

"In the poor box."

"No way."

He nods several times. "All of them rolled together like that. It must have been from one person."

A thousand dollars is a lot of money to donate. Most people would want a receipt. Or at least a thank-you note. I would.

On a typical week we average about twelve dollars in the poor box. Hence, its name.

Not today. One thousand dollars in tidy, new bills.

Jim has to sit down. "Why do people do things like this?" he complains. "It's such a shock. Why can't they just write checks and send them in the mail like regular folks?"

I nod and make sympathetic noises.

Jim wipes his brow and locks the money inside the desk drawer, which helps him recover some of his usual calm.

"It was probably someone who won the lottery, or something," he reasons, sitting back in the desk chair. "Or maybe they got lucky at cards."

"Say, Jim . . ." I ponder out loud. "Do you remember that armored truck that overturned on I-94 last month? The newspaper said that a bunch of motorists stopped and helped gather up the money . . ."

He bolts straight out of his chair. "No! They wouldn't—they couldn't! Why give it to us? We're just an ordinary thrift store!"

13

Thrifty Givers

O ne of my occasional tasks at St. Vincent de Paul is
to write thank-you notes to our donors. As with
everything else at the store, I don't do this alone. Walter,
our current president, composes the majority of them,
and when he's too busy, he calls on several of our other
members. These people are all volunteers themselves,
who rarely get thanked, but they know how important
gratitude is. They send letters to anyone who writes us
a check for any amount. We don't have the resources to
send notes to everyone who hands us a twenty, but we do
post our thanks in the church bulletin after we take up
special collections.

I mostly write notes to the people who donate nice furniture or appliances. We appreciate nice things because
our customers and clients appreciate them. If someone
gives us a ratty, broken-down sofa covered with pet hair,
we thank them politely, but we do not send notes in the
mail. If, however, the donation was obviously something
that the person cared for and kept in nice condition, and
I have their name and address, I try to send them our
appreciation.

One day, a fierce-eyed woman strides into the store and demands to see "the management." That turns out to be me by virtue of everyone else pointing their fingers in my direction. The lady is upset. She donated money to us in memory of a recently deceased friend, and the friend's children have not received a thank-you note from us.

I am taken aback. "Didn't you receive a note from us?" I ask.

"Yes, yes, of course, with a tax receipt attached. But the family doesn't know that I gave the money because you didn't send *them* any kind of acknowledgement."

"Umm . . . how would we know their address?"

"Well, the funeral home must have given it to you when they gave you my check."

I think I see the problem. "Oh, but we only send a thank-you to the donor's address," I explain calmly. "But, don't worry. The funeral home will send the family a list of all the people who donated through them. Your friend's family should get something soon that shows you gave money to us."

She literally stamps her foot at me. "I don't care what they got from the funeral home. You people should have sent a thank-you note! This is a terrible way to take people's money. No credit given where credit is due. I am very unhappy."

I am very baffled.

But I make use of Dorothy's best phrase for irate customers. "I'm sorry this didn't work out the way you hoped. How can we make it right?"

Her face is flushed, and her eyebrows are set disapprovingly, but her volume comes down a notch. "You need to send her children a proper thank-you note telling them that I gave twenty-five dollars in their mother's name. It's just common courtesy. A legitimate organization would have done it weeks ago."

I go into the office and pull out a notepad. She recites the address to me, and I assure her that we will put our written gratitude in the mail forthwith. She leaves only slightly mollified.

I am half-inclined to send her twenty-five dollars back to her, but I swallow my irritation and write a nice note to her friend's family and slap on a stamp.

The mission of the St. Vincent de Paul Society is not only to help people in need, but it is also to help other people help the needy.

For some reason, this is the very hardest part for me.

One rainy Michigan day, I arrive to open the shop at nine in the morning. There is no place to park my car, but it's not due to a rush of customers or clients. All the parking slots are filled with furniture. I pull up crosswise in front of a jumble of soaked sofas, put on my flashers, and climb out of the car. Gene is standing in the open back door, arms crossed, glumly staring at the full lot.

I spread my hands. "What is all this?"

"What is it? It's seven sofas, six broken end tables, a stove without a door, three entertainment centers, and two television sets."

"All of them wet," I say, aiming a disgusted foot at the nearest muddy cushions. "What are we going to do with it all? It will fill up our dumpster ten times. I can't believe how inconsiderate people are—why would they do this to a charity?"

Gene nods his head. "Calm down. I already called our trash hauler and explained the situation. They said they'd come pick it all up for the cost of one dumpster."

"Did they really? That's awfully good of them."

Gene shrugs. "It's a funny world when the garbage men are more charitable than the people who make donations."

My husband, Dean, is inexplicably not troubled by slacker donors. He sees taking care of their junk as an opportunity to teach people how to help those in need. It seems to me that he's way nicer than necessary, and that people can learn from a good scolding just as easily.

On Saturday, Dean goes out to pick up donated furniture and appliances with a couple of the high school students. Their first stop is a tiny post-WWII tract house. The owners are a young couple with a baby on the way. This is their first house. They are preparing for the arrival of their little one, but the previous owners left a large freezer in the basement that is taking up the space they need for a washer and dryer. They want to donate it to St. Vincent de Paul.

Our three crew members follow the young man into the basement, duck down under the basement stairs, and find an appliance that is not only older than the high school kids, it's older than Dean. It looks like a bloated, rusty, chrome-adorned coffin with a turquoise lining.

The two students bend over and heft one end to test its weight. These kids are football players, but after a couple of attempts, they stand back and eye the monster freezer and the narrow staircase with a solemn loss of faith.

Dean, sensing a teaching moment, gives them a confidence building pep talk. He pulls out a screwdriver and cheerfully shows them how to remove the hand railing on the stairs, the exterior door on the house, and the screen door. After they have made the exit path as barrier-free as possible, all four of them gather under the stairs and divide up around the corners of the freezer.

"Okay, on three," Dean says, and begins the count. The first of many counts.

The way Dean describes it to me later that day, it would have gone a little smoother if they had removed the lid of the freezer before it got stuck on the landing. And it would have helped if he'd been wearing gloves when his hand got pinched between the doorjamb and the chrome trim. And it was probably best that the monster dropped on his foot when they lifted it onto the truck, rather than on one of the student's feet.

"Uh-huh," I say, while preparing a fresh bag of ice. "Did the couple give you any money for gas?"

He winces as I apply the compress. "They're just starting out. We can afford gas for the truck better than they can"

I sigh. "You didn't take that old freezer to the store, did you?"

"It was worthless. I had to pay the guy at the dump thirty dollars to take it off our hands."

"Hmph. It could have been worse, I suppose."

He grins at me and winks. "I told the young couple that you would send them a receipt in the mail."

I am getting to be a grump.

Not with the people we are helping—they pretty much have me infatuated. By now I have learned the lesson not to judge the people seeking help because their circumstances often fill me with a keening empathy, and they teach me how lucky I am, and how ungrateful I have been.

It's the donors who inflame my indignation.

Intellectually, I recognize that this is a form of judging-my-neighbor. I also know that what annoyed Jesus the most when he walked this earth was we self-righteous, church-going folks who find flaws in everyone else and none in ourselves.

Even so. Give me this one. These people can be clueless.

I do a fair job of burying my grumpiness beneath smiles and thank-you notes, all the while wondering what the remedy can be. It appears in a little old man.

He steps into the store, moving slowly with his cane, and inquires if we will take some donated clothing. Of course, we will. He has it in his car—can we help unload it?

I walk with him out to the parking lot and am almost immediately overwhelmed by the sight. He opens up a minivan, filled to the ceiling, back to front, with bags of clothing.

"It's rather a lot," he apologizes. "If you don't want so much, maybe you can tell me where else I could take it?"

I realize that he has seen my dismay, and I quickly retrench. "Oh, this is no problem. We always need new clothing. Just give me a minute to find a place to put it in the back room, alright?"

"Well, none of it is new, I'm afraid," he says. "It's my wife's things. She died a few weeks ago, and I know she would have wanted it to go to a charity, so I thought of this place. You're sure it's not too much?"

My grumpiness melts. I offer sympathy and condolences and ask his wife's name. He lights up when he sees I am interested. I tell him how we help poor people and that the clothing will find good homes. He is consoled by the thought of someone else needing the things, as many people are. He opens one of the bags to show me how nice the things are, what good condition they are in. Many people do this, but this time I am amazed.

All the items have been freshly laundered and smell of fabric softener. He has sorted the clothing types and labeled the outside of all the bags with the contents. The woolens have dry-cleaner wrappers and the shoes have all been polished.

The nightgowns are ironed.

I say to him as we finish hauling in the last bag. "You must have taken very good care of your wife when she was sick. I have never seen clothing so beautifully prepared."

His lower lip quivers, but he smiles his acknowledgment.

I have fresh hope. Jesus has not given up on me yet. Apparently he still sees in me someone who he might be able to save.

14

FLYING THE SAME
PLANE

There is more than one kind of peace. And every kind worth its salt is marked by an absence of fear.

But fear is something that's hard for me to forgo. Somewhere along the way in my adulthood, I've grown fond of expressing my little anxieties. Even more than most people, I like to worry out loud about foul weather, the roads, the holidays, and the air traffic around Chicago. For me, a good dose of self-righteous stress over unleashed dogs or the state of the educational system is not so much a habit as a hobby.

At St. Vincent de Paul we often see fear in the eyes of the people who come to us for help—fear of eviction, fear of utility shutoff, fear we won't be able to help them. It's amazing how gratitude zaps it. Fear will so often retreat where there is thankfulness.

"Thank you, Jesus!" a client whoops when I tell him that we will be able to prevent him from being evicted. The wrinkles on his forehead disappear, he sits back in the chair, and he lets out a huge sigh, overflowing with relief.

This man, and many of the people we help, cannot afford the luxury of getting worked up over things like endangered species and liability insurance. They have in-your-face problems in spades. Why take on more?

Dorothy sums it up beautifully when I ask her why she has worked so many years at the St. Vincent de Paul shop.

"I always go home grateful," she tells me. "After listening to all the troubles that our clients have to deal with, my problems look small."

This may be okay for someone in their eighties with few responsibilities, but it doesn't seem like a workable solution for my anxieties. Our client's problems are often monstrous, true, but that doesn't seem like a good enough reason to let go of my own.

Then, one Friday, after we close, someone breaks into the store.

First, they slam the glass in the front door and find out it's constructed with that intention in mind. Only large cracks appear. Next, they go around to the side of the building and try to pry open the steel exit door. They bend it, but it won't budge. They finally manage to enter by way of the garage door into the back room, tearing up the bottom panel. When they get in, they smash the cash register and extract twenty dollars, which they make away with.

It is unsettling for Jim when he arrives on Saturday to find all the broken doors. He makes a phone call, and the police come. They take notes and dust for fingerprints and scold Jim for entering the building. He thanks them, cleans up the glass, and opens the store for business.

"Customers were waiting to come in," he explains to me later.

"What about the broken cash register?" I ask. "How could you ring up sales?"

"Luckily, the drawer was stuck open. We left it that way all day. The customers were patient about it."

The customers are also furious that such a thing would happen to us. One of them says to me, "Put a sign on the door saying you won't be giving any money away until the burglars' identities are given to the police. They'll have them within a week."

That's a tempting idea. I think about it for a second or two. We could punish the clients who need help by withholding charity until the thief is caught. Or not caught.

"Nah," I answer. "We can't let this stop us from being who we are. Giving money away is what the St. Vincent de Paul Society does. Thank goodness they stole so little."

Margaret, one of our volunteers, suggests that we post this sign: *Instead of breaking in for money, come in during our regular business hours and ask nicely for it.*

Even though most of our volunteers are defenseless old ladies, not one expresses any fear for their personal safety. The episode doesn't even take up much of our prayer time at the next meeting. "It's happened before," Alice says with a shrug. "What a blessing that nobody was here."

What a blessing? Does she really mean that?

Apparently so. I watch in amazement while everyone goes back to discussing the pricing and sorting of used clothing as if the break-in is already old news. I think we should spend time talking about burglar alarms, hidden panic buttons, and emergency procedures. I have just spent an hour sweeping up fingerprint powder, and no one has given me a chance to express any real anxiety over it. I feel cheated.

Not for long.

The next time I am at the store, Dorothy sticks her head in the office where I am working and says, "Jane, I think you better come—we don't know what to do with this fellow out here." She looks nervously over her shoulder.

Four volunteers are working the floor of the St. Vincent de Paul shop. This is an over-abundance of help compared to most days, which is why I am in the office.

I am in the middle of interviewing a middle-aged gentleman who is considering joining our charitable work. He looks healthy and strong and forty years younger than our average volunteer. I'm thinking that he will be perfect for handling these occasional troublesome customers. I am eager to recruit him because of my own fear of being the one that the older ladies call on to deal with the unruly types.

But not yet. I don't want to scare him off by introducing him to the tough cases too soon.

I start to hint to Dorothy that four ladies should be able to help one customer, when Fran appears and adds her anxieties to the mix. "Jane, we can't handle this man. You need to come deal with him. He's loud, he's really tall, and he's soaking wet."

The new volunteer I am interviewing sits up straighter in his chair and asks her, "What's he doing?"

"He's in the dressing room." Dorothy says. "We found him some clothes, and he's trying them on."

Fran heads for the back room. "Oh, dear, I better get him a plastic bag to put his wet things in."

Our new volunteer says confidently, "Looks like you ladies can use some help. I'll talk with him." He stands up and walks out on the floor, and I follow him. He approaches our dressing room and speaks through the curtain. "Hey, man, why don't you let me help you find some clothes?"

The voice from within says loudly, "Dude, you and me don't fly the same plane. The ladies are doing just fine."

The ladies' eyes pop, but grins appear where worry lines had been. Fran pushes a plastic bag under the curtain and says, "Put your wet clothes in this, Sir."

Alice brings two pairs of dry socks and underwear and places those next to the bag.

The voice from within booms, "I love you Catholic ladies! I knew you would take care of me."

Marilyn calls out from the clothing racks, "I found another pair of pants that might fit."

The curtain flies back to reveal a dry, happy, young man. "It's so cold out there, I'll wear them both. Woo-hoo—you ladies dress me *good*!"

He leaves the shop wearing double layers and toting a bag with soap, razor, mittens, and bagels. The ladies have a good laugh at themselves.

Later, in my own neighborhood, I am walking my dog, Trixie, a fourteen-year-old mongrel with more moxie than muscle. In the distance, a pit bull appears, running loose. My heart rate increases immediately. I have experienced this scene before. I know how it will end.

The loose dog will come charging up to us while I shout and pull Trixie away by her leash. Trixie will slip her head out of the collar (she has a thick neck and small ears) and she will bite the other dog. In the face, if possible. Then Trixie will get knocked down, and I will scream and throw sticks and eventually, if I'm lucky, the dog's owner will come running up and lead the bloodied dog away. Trixie will be mostly fine because she has really thick fur all over her, especially around her neck, but I will be rattled and upset. I will exchange angry words with the other owner, and world peace will be set back a notch.

But this time is different. Because of St. Vincent de Paul, I have been thinking more and more about the badness of fear. I know I will never get rid of all the loose dogs in the world so I have decided to read some books to help me get over my fear of loose dogs. Hurrah for Cesar Milan. He has taught me to think as a dog thinks. His books have shown me the signals dogs give to each other with their actions, their body language, and their eye contact.

He tries to teach people how to fly the same plane that dogs are flying.

So as this dog approaches at a dead run, I grip Trixie's leash firmly, tell her to "heel," and we take two decisive steps in the direction of the charging pit bull.

The dog comes to a sudden stop. Hurrah for Ce—

The dog starts charging us again.

We take two more fast steps in his direction.

He stops. This time, instead of charging us, he takes two steps toward us.

We mimic him.

Two steps at a time, by turns, we approach each other in this halting manner. I keep my mouth shut and my elbows pinned to my side. Trixie and the other dog both have their tails raised high in the "I'm the alpha dog here" signal. I'm still sure that someone is going to get bitten, but I'm fighting this fear with all my strength.

The two dogs sniff noses. I hold my breath.

The pit bull lays down in front of Trixie. The sign of submission. Hurrah for Cesar Milan!

After a few minutes, they sniff each other over politely, and Trixie and I continue on our walk.

(Do not try this at home. I was lucky the other dog was a very young animal and that Trixie kept her temper.)

But back at St. Vinnie's, I begin to appreciate the wisdom of my co-volunteers. They are working in a rough neighborhood. No doubt about it. They have their fears about this, yet they don't approach the work fearfully. They approach it two steps at a time, facing forward all the while. They don't shout and wave their arms, nor do they throw sticks or blame other people.

If I live without giving in to fear, will all loose dogs lie down in submission? No. But some of them will.

If the St. Vincent de Paul Society continues its work without giving in to fear, will we all be perfectly safe? Maybe not. But it's worked so far. Who am I to change their methods?

This way, at least, we're all flying the same plane.

15

NOT MY POOR PEOPLE

One of our longtime donors, a person who regularly sends us large checks, telephones us at the shop one day. "Jane," she says in an agitated voice, "Tell me what you do when someone comes up to you on the street and asks for a handout."

"Um . . . back up a minute. I'm guessing this happened to you?"

"Yes. Again today. It makes me feel awful. This woman came up to me while I was on my way to a meeting downtown, and she asked if I could spare a few dollars. I shook my head at her and kept walking, and now I feel terrible. I mean, this lady looked like she needed the money—she wasn't asking for much—but what if she wanted to use it for alcohol or drugs? What if she asks me again tomorrow, and again, and again? Aren't there places she can go? Should I have sent her to St. Vincent de Paul? I never know what to do in these situations! What do you do?"

I squirm and tell her my feeble method. "I take five dollars out of my purse and put it in my pocket before I go to work at St. Vincent de Paul. If someone asks for it, I give it to them. Once it's gone, it's gone. I sort of leave it up to God. But the big money has to come from the St. Vincent de Paul Society. My pocket isn't deep enough."

I remind her of the Good Samaritan story. The Samaritan is not the only hero in the messy business of the man who was mugged on the highway. A careful reading will reveal that it's the innkeeper who actually does the work of taking care of the hapless traveler. The Good Samaritan gives some preliminary help and foots the bill, sure, but the innkeeper is put in charge of the long-term effort.

"Remember," I tell our generous donor. "The Good Samaritan didn't stick around, but he told the innkeeper something like, "Whatever you spend, I'll repay you." Which is kind of what you do for us nearly every month, right?"

"Yeah . . . so I should send people to St. Vinnie's?"

"Because you support us financially, that makes you the Samaritan and St. Vincent de Paul plays the part of the innkeeper. The parable shows a need for both immediate assistance and a long-term refuge. As far as panhandlers go, you should certainly feel free to send people here anytime."

"Okay, I will," she says. "But I'll think about putting a five in my pocket too."

Our generous donor raises an interesting question. She has already gotten beyond the "Am I my brother's keeper?" issue with a resounding yes. Now, her problem is, when am I my brother's keeper?

Once a month, or any given day?

All of my brothers?

Whether they deserve it or not?

I struggle with this too. After more than a year working at the St. Vincent de Paul shop, I still keep looking for "the deserving poor"—the innocent ones who are blatant victims of injustice and hard luck. I want to help them and no one else.

From what I can see, apart from children, most poor people's situations seem to stem from a mixture of uncontrollable circumstances, luck, and their own decisions. Same as my situation.

Do I deserve everything I have? Am I somehow more moral, smarter, or a harder worker than poor people? Sometimes I am, most times I'm not.

Do poor people deserve their daily struggle for existence? Are they immoral, stupid, and lazy? Sometimes they are, most times they aren't.

A telemarketer calls our St. Vincent de Paul shop a few days before Thanksgiving.

The young man asks if we are located near Lawton, Michigan.

Walter, who answers the phone, admits that we are.

The telemarketer explains that he is calling from Tennessee, and goes on to tell him about a phone call he placed earlier that morning.

"I dialed an elderly lady who lives in Lawton, and she is in the middle of one awful mess. Her kitchen faucet won't shut off, and the sink drain is plugged. She's been hauling the water out of her house in a bucket for three days nonstop. She hasn't slept, and the water is gaining on her."

Walter is a little slow on the uptake. "You're a telemarketer? And you're calling from where?"

"Tennessee," he repeats patiently. "You see I knew the St. Vincent de Paul Society helps with out-of-the-ordinary problems, and you have the same area code as Lawton. If I give you her name and address, would you all check on her? She's ninety-four years old and says she hasn't got a soul to help."

Walter thanks the young man and then dials Fred, an experienced Vincentian from Battle Creek, the next town east of us, to ask him for advice.

Fred pauses a moment after hearing the unusual tale. "Well, doesn't that beat all?" he says. "It just so happens that my son is a building contractor, and he's working at the Lawton High School today. I'll call him on his cell phone."

Fred's son finds the house on his lunch break and also finds things worse than described. The exhausted lady is up to her ankles in water, and the plumbing system needs more salvation than a building contractor carries in his truck. He phones a local firm, which dispatches two plumbers, who take seven-and-a-half hours to put things in order. Their bill to the St. Vincent de Paul Society is only $360, the cost of materials.

Fred's son invites the lady to his home for Thanksgiving dinner, and introduces her to some nice folks who she can call when she's in a fix.

And the telemarketer? He never did tell anyone what he was selling. But he took responsibility for a stranger in a modern-day twist on the Good Samaritan. Would anyone have known about it if he had politely wished her a good day and hung up the phone? Could he have gotten in trouble at work for taking the time to look up our number and calling us? Do I have a new respect for telemarketers?

France is a wealthy country, I remind myself as I walk the cobbled streets of Lille on a trip with Dean. Not only wealthy, but its government has strong social supports in place. They have systems to take care of the poor that put our American poverty-reduction programs to shame.

And yet there are panhandlers on the street corners, just like in the United States.

On my first trip out of our hotel alone, I keep my hands jammed inside the pockets of my raincoat and walk past a toothless man who is holding out a paper cup. He is standing silently in front of the sandwich shop, eyes searching each customer's face. I pretend not to notice him.

My reasoning goes like this: I spend a lot of volunteer hours working for the St. Vincent de Paul Society. There are plenty of poor people back in Michigan who need my coins, and this man with the cup is not my poor person. He is the French people's poor person. They are perfectly capable of taking care of their own.

At the next corner a young man approaches and asks in French if I have some coins to spare.

"No polly voo Fransay," I tell him convincingly. He switches to Spanish, then English. It's difficult to imagine a trilingual poor person in the United States. I walk on.

The small family at the end of the block makes me pause (they are blocking the sidewalk). The father is play-ing the accordion, the mother rattles her tambourine, and their young son dances with his small fiddle. The child, about eight years old, is dressed in an embroidered

red felt vest, knickers, and shiny black shoes. A brass spittoon is displayed prominently on a bandana with coins glinting inside and around it.

The kid is cute, the music is entertaining, and these are definitely not my poor people. I watch for a brief moment and then continue on to my destination for the day, a museum called Musee de l'Hospice Comtesse, loosely translated as Hospital of the Countess.

In thirteenth-century France, only the rich could afford to receive proper health care. In medieval times the poor had many burdens, and the wealthy had the burden of caring for the poor. Like today, not all the rich took this obligation personally, but the countess who provided the funds to build this hospital for the destitute had been immortalized by the museum I was visiting.

As I take the tour and listen to the long history of charity that has taken place here, I realize that God doesn't distinguish between us, rich or poor, French or American, socialist or capitalist. All are his rich people and all are his poor people.

As I leave the museum, I feel for the coins in my pocket.

Maybe the family of street musicians is still there . . .

16

FOUR WOMEN

I am sometimes aware of my own motives. I have secretly hoped it might be possible to get to heaven by learning all I need to know through reading books and articles. After only a short time at St. Vincent de Paul, I can see now where that may not be the way it works. Juris Rubenis, a Latvian pastor, wrote, "Theology is talking about God when God is not in the room."

I recognize that situation. I've been in that room. It's comfortable.

Well, the St. Vincent de Paul shop seems to be more like talking with God when he is not only in the room, but he smells, and cries, and prefers to do all the talking himself. It's this type of messiness that I have spent considerable effort to avoid.

There are times when I see the suffering around the world and around our town, and I just plain look in the other direction.

When earthquakes strike in remote places, a call goes out for search-and-rescue teams, medical personnel, and the military. It is not a coincidence that I chose to teach math as a career. As far as I know, there has never been an emergency call put out for the immediate assistance of the nation's geometry teachers.

I am perfectly willing to put a check in the mail to whatever group is responding, perfectly content to let them handle it. I prefer to help people when they are calm, courteous, and grateful. I say to myself, "After they get things cleaned up, after the chaos is under control, if they need to learn a little about the Pythagorean theorem then I'm on it."

Within a week, four women come through the door of the St. Vincent de Paul Society. Each of them is facing homelessness, and their stories are the messy kind that do not respond well to geometric logic. I am in high-avoidance mode.

The first is a widow who has two teenagers to support on a part-time income. She is sweet and grateful and gets teary-eyed as she tells me about the many people who have helped her. But in the fog of grief—both hers and the children's—she hasn't been able to find the type of job she needs to pay the bills. She is stuck in despair, can't go back to school, can't fill out job applications, and can't move out of a house that is too much work and too much money.

"I just haven't been able to figure out finances," she explains. "My husband used to do all that, and I don't understand it."

I nod sympathetically as I fill in the paperwork. "When did you lose your husband?"

"Fifteen years ago."

I stop writing. *Oh, my.*

This woman is not just a little depressed. She is not going to be helped by a few encouraging words and some extra money for the mortgage. Her situation is way beyond my kind of help.

I revert to my geometry-teacher mode and call in the rescue squad. "Have you told your doctor about that?"

She looks confused. "Why would I tell my doctor about my finances?"

"I think he may have some ideas, that's all. Doctors know a lot."

The second woman calls us on the phone and sobs out a story of a drug-addicted husband who has stolen money from her parents, causing her to lose their trust. He then spent all the mortgage money on his drugs, and after that, in a rage, he broke her hand.

"I can't drive; the doctor put a pin in the bone, and they told me not to use my hand at all. I don't know what to do. They told me not to lift over five pounds, but I have a baby and a two-year-old."

"Hold on, hold on," I say in a not-so-calming voice. "Where is your husband right now?"

"He's in jail. The hospital called the sheriff because he went domestic on me."

"He went domestic?" I am confused.

"Yeah. They charged him with domestic because he broke my hand."

"Oh. Good. That's good." I take a breath. "And where are you?"

"I'm home with the babies. But I don't have any money—it's all too much!"

Too much for me too.

I tell her the number of the local women's shelter. "You need to call these people. They know how to help you. If after you've seen them, you still need some money for the bills, call us back, okay?"

"Okay," she whimpers, "thanks."

The third lady is working two jobs, yet still facing eviction and an empty pantry. I arrange to visit her at work because she can't afford to take time off to ask for help. She is a greeter at a local big box store: one of those people who stand in the drafty doorway all day, saying, "Welcome to _____." And "Have a nice day!"

It is four-thirty in the afternoon before I can arrange to meet her. I walk in the second entrance as instructed and spot a fiftyish woman wearing a red scarf, just like she said she would. I approach her with my clutch of paperwork and say, "Hi. I'm Jane from St. Vincent de Paul. Are you Lucille?"

She looks relieved and embarrassed. "This is so nice of you to meet me here. I didn't know how I was going—;" she smiles over my shoulder, "Welcome to _____." She reaches behind her and yanks out a shopping cart for the customer. "Here you go, Sir."

I have taken a couple of steps aside so as not to interfere. The man looks at me briefly and moves on. My client smiles broadly and says, "Have a nice day!" to someone who is walking out the door.

I look around to see if anyone else is approaching from either direction, and quickly say to Lucille, "Do you have a break time soon, when we could talk?"

She shakes her head. "Have a nice day, Ma'am! Not until I get off work at eight, and then I have to go to my night job. Welcome to _____! Can you just get what you need from me here? Welcome to _____! Do you need a cart?"

I unfold the papers and pull a pen out of my purse. "I'm going to need your landlord's name and phone number, your address, and the last four digits of your Social Security."

"Have a nice day! His name is _____ and he lives on _____. Have a nice day! And my Social Security number is _____. Need a cart today, Miss?"

I would start giggling except Lucille doesn't think it's funny. She is worried because her boss might spot us, and she could get fired for fraternizing with a charity that helps underemployed people. She wipes away tears of anger as she looks warily around for signs of her employer. We finish the paperwork in a rudimentary way. I give her a promise of some money and the name of a church that helps people over the phone. "Call these folks and tell them you already spoke with us." I shove the papers in my pocket and she says, "Thanks so much— Welcome to _____!" And I escape from her world as swiftly as humanly possible.

The fourth woman I see this week is already living on the street. She is unnaturally thin and wears her hair in a long, limp ponytail. She has no appointment to see us and nearly walks away when we ask if she does. We call her back and with a little prompting find out what she wants. All she asks for is warm clothing and a blanket. We give her that, and she turns to go.

The first three women apologized to me for their tears. They were trying their best to cope, but life seemed to go from bad to worse. When I gave the small comfort of a listening ear, the widow responded by pouring out her feelings of profound shock; the second one's voice shook with fear; and the third was just plain angry.

"It's okay," I told them. "In your situation, I would cry too."

The fourth lady, the one who wants a blanket, is past crying. She doesn't appear to care at all what happens to her next. I ask what other assistance we can offer her. "Nothing," she says. She takes the clothing and the blanket, politely thanks me, and leaves the store with the same blank expression she came in with.

It is not a good thing when someone is so easily helped. It is not good when the poor are silent. It is her face that haunts me at night, hers that I remember.

Slowly, I am beginning to realize that I prefer tears to resignation. I prefer shouting, anger, and bitterness to a courteous hopelessness. I would rather deal with someone's mess than with their silence, because there is no way to clean up silence.

It must be I was never meant to discuss theology.

I prefer to talk about God when God is in the room.

17

ECHOES OF CHRISTMAS

It is late fall when Gloria, a Vincentian from the outer diocese, calls me. She tells me the story of a young couple, unmarried, nine months pregnant, who walked all the way across town to ask for help from their St. Vincent de Paul group. (Hmm . . . it's beginning to feel a lot like Christmas . . .)

They needed a ride to get an ultrasound. With no family support, they were facing the birth of their first child alone and penniless. First thing Gloria did was take them out to eat. Next she registered them with a pregnancy counseling service. After those two essential steps, the St. Vincent team visited them at their home, a rundown rental that was cold and legally uninhabitable. Neither the kitchen appliances nor the furnace worked. There was no crib nor much in the way of other furniture either.

It may as well have been a stable.

Gloria's team called the city's building inspector, who made a list of fix-it-or-else items for the landlord.

The reason Gloria was calling me was that with the birth expected any day, she was putting out a request to other Vincentian groups for baby necessities. We searched the store shelves and soon they had a crib, a car seat, a stroller, a layette, and even winter coats for mom and dad.

Because the neighborhood where they lived was one where taxis refused to come in the middle of the night, Gloria gave the young couple her cell phone number and told them to call her when labor started. Grateful is too weak a word for how this family felt. Two days later, Gloria got the call and ordered up an ambulance courtesy of the St. Vincent de Paul Society.

After the baby's arrival, the extended family members began to pull together. They pooled their resources and brought the young couple a stove and a refrigerator and joined in the celebration of new life.

"We'll keep an eye on them," Gloria promises when she calls us again. "He's finishing his GED and taking computer classes—he's no slacker. They're not married because the money just isn't there, but we'll work on that." She pauses. "Next up is Christmas. We'll see that they get one."

I don't doubt it. A struggling young couple, a newborn babe and a "Gloria"—hmmm . . . Add a few gifts from afar and a whole lot of *in excelsis Deo*—and everything is good to go.

When Jesus blessed the five loaves and two fish and instructed his friends to share it with the crowd, it still looked like five loaves and two fish. They must have felt a bit foolish telling everyone to sit down and dig in. They couldn't have known that the miracle would only occur after they gave the food away.

At our planning meeting in November, Walter, our president, informs us that the checkbook is low, sales in the store are off, requests for Christmas baskets are way up, and several of our key members are leaving over the holidays. Our dilemma is this: do we give away meager baskets, turn away some of the requests, or just drop the whole Christmas-basket effort?

We struggle with it. Isn't it more important to help with rent and utility bills than with Christmas gifts? Some of the same people ask for our baskets every year— should we say "no" to them? Many clients sign up with us because we give gift certificates for food along with the toys for the kids—we could cut off the food, or maybe the toys? Should families with teenagers receive gifts too? How will we find enough helpers to collect, sort, and wrap the gifts?

In the end, looking at our five loaves and two fish, we shrug our shoulders and decide to take requests as usual and do what we can.

The day we put the baskets together, more volunteers show up than we have counter space to put them to work. Several large monetary donations arrive in the mail that afternoon, and we have so many toys left over that we go across the street to the homeless family shelter and give them baskets too.

Just as we are cleaning up, Walter hands me the names and ages of two children. Their mom, struggling to pay the electric bill, has returned their gifts to Wal-Mart three days before Christmas because she needs the cash. She is crying in our office.

We send her home with a bag worthy of St. Nick.

Our worrying was such a waste of time.

18

COOL

The woman in front of me doesn't look at all healthy, and she isn't. "I've got cancer," she says bluntly. "The doctors say it's inoperable, and I don't think it's fair to ask them how long I have. That's not something I need to know anyway. What I want to know is, will you take me as a volunteer?"

Earlier that morning, at the beginning of our shift, we had prayed for more volunteers to help with all the heavy lifting and the long days in the store.

The woman in front of me explains that the cancer is in her lungs and her bones and most of her organs. She doesn't have a lot of strength or energy, but she would really like to help out.

She isn't strong enough to lift boxes of clothing or push furniture around. Even the bags of bread look too heavy for her. The only thing I can figure is that if God sent this woman to us, then he must have his reasons. But pray-ers can't be choosers. Compassion for down-trodden people is the only qualification a person needs to work at St. Vincent de Paul. Good health is merely an option.

"My name's Christine," she says and puts out her hand. It shows the bruises from I.V. lines, and I am afraid I will hurt her if I squeeze her fingers.

Perhaps we can put her to work answering our constantly ringing phone. At the very least, she is being straightforward so I follow her lead. "Cool," I say and lightly grasp her outstretched hand. "Welcome to St. Vinnie's."

A smile as big as a sunrise.

"When can I start?" she asks.

"How about today?"

My quick invitation catches her off guard, but she is just as quick to accept. "I never know if there will be a tomorrow—so why not today?" She rolls up her sleeves and pitches in sorting clothing.

Christine has been a realtor most of her life, she tells us, but because of her illness she is now living on disability. Many of her former customers have been calling, begging her to help them sell their houses. It's not news to us that the mortgage crisis is catching a lot of people who never in their lives thought they would be in a housing emergency. "It's really sad," she says. "I wish I could help them but I'm just not up to it."

I tell Christine that a woman is coming to see us later that day about an eviction, and ask if she would like to be part of the team helping.

"Cool," she says.

An hour later, Christine and I sit down in our small office with a middle-aged woman who has taken her lunch hour from work to come tell us her problems.

Our client, a mother of seven, is in a messy situation with her landlord, who seems intent on clearing the apartment complex and starting over again with new tenants. She is up to date with her rent, but there has been a questionable complaint filed against one of her children, followed by a series of coercive manipulations aimed at getting her to vacate before her lease is up. She is unhappy living under this constant pressure, but it isn't easy finding housing for seven children. On top of that, she doesn't have any money put aside for moving expenses and is afraid she won't get her security deposit back because of all the ill will between her and the landlord.

This is way beyond anything I know how to help with—but not beyond our brand-new volunteer. Christine asks to look over the lease and the complaints and, after reading them carefully, she tells our client what rights she has and which battles are worth fighting. They discuss options for finding other housing, a reasonable timetable, and how to negotiate a fair solution. I listen to the whole discussion and take notes for future cases I might run into.

Very cool.

Christine leaves at the end of the day with a happy-tired face and a promise to return.

Our client comes back two weeks later with a lease for a new home where her kids can remain in their same schools and where they have a yard to play in for the first time in their lives. Cool.

I visit the funeral home the following week. Christine's family tells me that she loved volunteering with us, and they have requested that memorials be made out to St. Vincent de Paul.

"Would that be okay?" they ask.

"Cool" is the only thing I can manage to say.

19

REPLANTING THE FOREST

When I started as a volunteer at the St. Vincent de Paul thrift shop, it was open three days a week. They lacked the volunteers to cover any more hours. That was one of the reasons I found myself joining the Society. Dorothy was the other.

Her warm and personal invitation in spite of my impatience and arrogance taught me three lessons about acquiring new volunteers:

1. People want to help where it's really needed.
2. People need to be asked—*in person.*
3. Critics may be prime recruits.

The store is now open from 9:00–3:00 Tuesday through Friday, and 9:00–1:00 on Saturday. How do we fill all those hours? We use Dorothy's recipe.

Our teenagers know they're needed. Who else has the muscles and energy to haul furniture on Saturday mornings? Many of them stick with us through their college years.

Our empty nesters and retirees know that helping pay someone's electric bill is no small thing and more satisfying than endless games of golf.

Then there are the newly bereaved, who need to be asked because they lack the energy to fill the void themselves. We also recruit people dealing with chronic illness who never get asked to help at other places because their own problems appear to be too much of a burden.

We go after the disaffected, the unchurched, or bitter Catholics, who think their help isn't wanted. One person I asked to join us said, "I've been looking for a reason like this to get back in the church."

I write these stories down because it can't be that they were meant for only my ears. I worry that they won't keep happening if I don't keep telling people about how God does his work in my little life. This worry, of course, is another sign of how miniscule my faith is—how weak my roots are.

Dorothy has been my mentor, my spiritual director, and the tree doctor for my personal careening redwood. She would pooh-pooh the very idea, but that is exactly how I see her. Because of her gentle invitation and her prodding me to take on tasks that stretched me beyond my comfort level, and the examples of her patience, her hard work, her openness and her prayers, she has inspired me to dare to hope to be just like her when I grow up.

I am a full-fledged Vincentian now. I have signed up for the newsletter, given out my phone number, and cleaned the restroom. My fellow workers have forgiven me for my initial arrogance, and they continue to forgive me every week for my busybody attempts to organize God's work for him. By intertwining their roots with mine, by struggling together with the practical mechanics of how best to help the poor, they have become for me the good, firm soil I need to stay erect in the forest.

I write these stories down for them so that we can better grow together in this unmapped woods, unworried by either the bramble patches blocking our way or the fallen tree trunks around us.

A Conversation with Author Jane Knuth

In getting involved with the thrift store, when did you first realize that you had embarked on a graced, if unpredictable, journey?

I kept telling myself that I wasn't actually getting involved—I was only helping out for a little while. Then the encounter with the woman from the chapter "A Street Theologian" convinced me that my depth of understanding of forgiveness, church, Scripture, and charity was about ankle deep.

I kept repeating her story to my family and friends until someone said, "Gee, Jane, you really ought to write that down."

Well, I'm a math teacher, not a writer, but it didn't seem likely that God would send that story just to me. It had to be meant for more people. So I wrote it down and passed it around to my fellow Vincentians. From there it circulated around until my friend Midge told me to send it to *St. Anthony Messenger* magazine.

After the story was printed, an acquaintance who had recently lost his son in a tragic way said to me, "Thank you for that story; it really helped me a lot." Each story led to another.

Is that a good definition of "a graced journey"?

What kind of impact did this work have on you emotionally? I ask only because I think a lot of people expect to become permanently depressed when they work with "the poor."

I'm the type of person who is more likely to become hard-hearted rather than depressed. It's another way to respond to immeasurable problems, and it's equally useless.

What our patron Saint Vincent de Paul teaches us is that by helping each other face-to-face, there is always something we can do, even if it's only to offer a listening ear, help pay a bill, or provide clean clothing. It's the love that is offered that matters most. That's what changes the world, because it changes *us*. Our job is not to solve all the problems; our job is to comfort, clothe, feed, and visit.

Is that enough? Some people would say no.

All I know is, if I weren't doing the little bit that I'm doing, then I would probably get more and more hard-hearted as the years go by. That's never going to help bring about the kingdom.

There is joy in this work. Giving money to a person who badly needs it is the best kind of fun. When I get to tell someone who is feeling like a failure that God loves them to pieces, goose bumps run down my arms. And, of course, there is the joy of laughing at my own foibles.

Has this work challenged your theology in any way? Has it challenged your image of God? And if so, how?

I'm not sophisticated enough to have a personal theology. It's difficult enough to figure out the one I was taught. Since the St. Vincent de Paul Society is Catholic, it fits me well.

As far as my image of God is concerned, I need to explain something about myself first.

My grandmother was a school teacher. My father was also a teacher, as were my closest aunt, my closest cousin, my sister, my nephew, and my niece. Most of my parents' friends were teachers. I am a teacher, and many of my friends are teachers. I grew up surrounded and loved by teachers. I love teachers.

For me, God is the greatest teacher of all. Frequently my prayers start out with, "God, you're going to have to explain this to me . . ."

The St. Vincent de Paul shop is an unconventional-looking classroom, but the faculty members are outstanding.

How do other people respond when they learn that you work with the St. Vincent de Paul Society?

Politely. Somewhat blankly. Most people know very little about the work of the Society, which is one of the reasons I wrote the book.

It's dangerous to generalize, but if you could apply only three adjectives to the people who come to the store needing help, what would they be?

Hmm . . . wounded . . . tired . . . tangled . . . ?

Has this work surprised you in any way?

My husband says that it has been a surprise how many non-Catholics—and even friends that don't go to church—have joined us in volunteering at St. Vincent's. There is something right about this work that goes beyond boundaries.

Has this involvement had any influence on your more private and personal devotional/prayer life?

I don't know. My life and my prayers have changed and grown in many ways in the past fifteen years. Would it have grown differently if I hadn't been part of St. Vincent de Paul? Probably, but there's no way to figure that out.

If you could explode one myth about the people who need assistance in our society, what would it be? That is, what would you like to better explain to those of us who don't see ourselves as poor and needy?

Very few people see themselves as poor and needy. Most of our clients describe their situation as "going through a rough patch." If I ask, "How are you today?" typically, a client who is facing financial ruin will answer, "Blessed, I'm blessed." Or "I'm just fine, thanks."

On the occasions when I encounter a person who tries to make me feel guilty, or who is blaming everyone in the world for their problems, or who makes me feel threatened, then they are usually not a nice person. There are middle class people and rich people who do those things too, and they are not nice people either.

The majority of the people we help are doing the best they know how, just like everyone else on the planet.

Can you imagine ways in which—in ordinary church–community life—we could better remember and attend to the people on the margins?

Sure. You always start with prayer. Do that for awhile and eventually God will have to answer. (He has kind of obligated himself to do that). Then you will find yourself in similar predicaments that I describe in the book. Then you will need to pray some more.

Is there anything else you'd like to say that you've not had a chance to say, through the stories or in this interview?

Oh, thanks for asking, but I think I've said enough for now.

ACKNOWLEDGMENTS

I need to thank everyone whose story is in this book. You won't recognize yourselves because of the disguises I created, but I remember you very well. So well, that I *needed* to write about you. You have been God's gift to me. I am a different and better person because you shared your struggles with us at the St. Vincent de Paul thrift shop. May God bless you always, and may God bless many people through your stories.

The first story I wrote down was for my fellow Vincentians who worked on the "Wednesday and Friday crews": Dorothy, Jane C., Bernie D., Gene, Jim, Bonnie, Argie, Pat, Mary Kay, Fran, Shirley, Dottie, Joan, Peggy, Sheila, Kim, and Deacon Bob. They all liked it, so I wrote some more. Walter, our president, sent the stories to the diocesan newspaper, *The Good News*, which launched a monthly column. This book would never have been written without all of their encouragement. I thank all the members of the St. Vincent de Paul Society who have been my spiritual classmates. They helped me understand what God is trying to teach us and straightened my path when the lessons were obscure.

My friend, Midge Sweeney, surprised me when she suggested that I should send a story to a magazine for publication. My respect for her is such that it was not possible for me to ignore her advice. I also thank the people at *St. Anthony Messenger* for printing the piece.

My writing buddies, Katie, Bess, Gretchen, Joyce, and Sheila, kept me going when I was discouraged by rejection slips. They also read and critiqued every chapter with insight and clarity.

I am grateful for Jane Cowan, Sheila Coppinger, Walter Brockmeyer, Joan Carey, and Luna Rose Harrington-Godsey who all read the manuscript and offered valuable advice.

Jon Sweeney helped me pull the stories into a narrative, and LaVonne Neff pointed me toward Loyola Press where, thanks to Vinita Wright, Joe Durepos, and Steve Connor, *Thrift Store Saints* grew into a book I could never have formed on my own. They are kind, astute, and generous people, and I am lucky to have worked with all of them.

My daughters, Ellen and Martha, know how to run a cash register, sort clothing, and load furniture onto a pick-up truck because of St. Vincent de Paul. They also know that family comes first and charity work comes second. Thank you, lovely daughters, for growing into people I admire very much, and for volunteering with me over the years.

My mom (who is also named Dorothy, and who also volunteers at the thrift store) clips all of my published stories and keeps them in a binder. She was my first teacher in volunteerism, and she's a beautiful example of lifelong spiritual formation.

My husband, Dean, is the first to read the stories. He understands what I'm trying to say even when I don't say it very well. He prevents me from becoming preachy, and he helps to suppress my math teacher voice. Everyone who reads this book should be grateful for that. In addition—as Tim guessed in chapter 11—he really is a "wonderful husband."

A BRIEF BACKGROUND ON THE SOCIETY OF ST. VINCENT DE PAUL

The thrift store featured in this book is based in Kalamazoo, Michigan. It is one of 391 stores in the United States operated by the Society of St. Vincent de Paul.

The Society of St. Vincent de Paul is an international Catholic organization made up of nearly 130,000 men and women dedicated to spiritual growth by serving those in need. Founded in Paris in 1833 by Frédéric Ozanam, the Society selected St. Vincent de Paul (1581–1660) as its patron for his deep faith and generosity toward the poor.

The Society believes in the dignity of the human person and identifies Jesus with the poor. In addition to operating thrift stores, the Society of St. Vincent de Paul provides a variety of services to those in need, including emergency financial assistance, disaster relief, food programs, medical assistance, and prison ministry. Members of the Society of St. Vincent de Paul, known as Vincentians, help some 12 million people annually.

To learn more about the Society of St. Vincent de Paul or to see how you can make a personal difference in the lives of the poor, visit **www.svdpusa.org**. Don't leave the thrift store yet—there's plenty more to do!

Visit **www.loyolapress.com/thrift-store** to:

- Learn more about Jane Knuth

- Watch videos featuring Jane as well as her "saint" friends, and view photos of the store

- Download free discussion and companion guides

- Read more soul-stirring stories from Jane